art

A HISTORY OF WESTERN ARCHITECTURE

A HISTORY OF

WESTERN ARCHITECTURE

Mary Louise King

Illustrated with photographs and diagrams

New York   Henry Z. Walck, Incorporated   1967

To John

Contents

Foreword

When my son announced that he had offered to give his school art class an illustrated lecture on architecture, I was impressed but skeptical. He had accompanied us to Europe when he was nine, and as far as I was aware his interest in architecture was limited to tall buildings. He liked heights and I did not. He had admired any tall structure in which he could climb to the top, and whatever we said about the architectural importance of other buildings seemed to have been wasted words.

To my surprise, from his collection of colored slides he made a selection of buildings that covered a range of cities and centuries and was fairly representative of the important historic styles of architecture. Although he was uncertain of the names of some styles, he pointed to architectural features, such as columns, arches, domes, and spires, that distinguish one style from another. His problem was how to say accurately what he knew about each building and to explain how one differed from another architecturally. What he wanted to say, and his arrangement of the slides, suggested certain categories of information. Purpose of a building was one; materials and construction was another; size and shape was a third. But his principal idea was that his classmates were more familiar with the appearance of buildings closer to home than those on his slides. The art class, we agreed, might find his talk more interesting if he could explain why the Capitol of the United States and the local bank looked something like a foreign architectural masterpiece they had never seen.

Time for research was limited. Slides of familiar buildings were not difficult to obtain, but although many books on architecture were available all seemed too technical or too scholarly for him to understand easily. When neither he nor I could discover a history of architecture written expressly for young people, this book had its beginning.

In the long, long history of architecture, certain structural developments and specific buildings have been of great and lasting significance. It is on these that I have concentrated, relating them to events in history that will be familiar to most readers and pointing out their influence on the design of well-known buildings in the United States. I have also tried to emphasize the role that the architect, whether famous or unknown, played in the development of the historic styles of architecture. His knowledge of materials and building techniques determined whether a building stood or collapsed, whether it was practical and convenient or quite the opposite, and whether it was a beautiful work in which people took pride and pleasure or an ugly building that depressed men's spirits. And because the history of architecture is centuries long, I have not treated contemporary developments, exciting as they are, in the detail some readers may wish.

It is my hope that readers of this book will gain some understanding of the history of architecture and some appreciation of what architects have tried to do because, like painting, sculpture, and music, architecture is a part of everyone's cultural heritage. I also hope that they will look around them with a fresh eye and have fun recognizing the ages-old features of the familiar buildings in which they spend so much of their lives.

1 *The Earliest Western Architecture*

People have always needed shelter—shelter from wind and rain, from heat and cold, from wild animals and human enemies. When primitive man moved out of the shelter of a natural cave, he built for himself a crude hut—man's first independent structure and in time he built shelters for other purposes: for worship, for the dead, for cattle and the storage of grain. Over the millenniums, man's knowledge of how to build—of structural techniques—grew slowly but steadily, and so did his understanding of the strengths and weaknesses of the materials with which he worked. Building methods and building materials, however, are only parts of the story of architecture. Man seems always to have had a sense of beauty as well as a sense of utility, and the history of architecture is also the record of man's attempts to build something more than practical shelters that stood up to wind and weather.

People were living in Egypt as long ago as 10,000 B.C. Five thousand years passed before their descendants learned how to farm and domesticate animals, and another fifteen hundred years were needed before Egyptians learned how to make pottery, paint vases, build boats, and work with metal. By then they were living in villages and worshiping a variety of local gods. When, about 3200 B.C., Egypt was united under the kings of the First Dynasty, the Egyptians were using a system of hieroglyphic writing, and a prehistoric culture had developed into an Egyptian civilization—one that would endure nearly three thousand years almost without change. It had taken nearly seven thousand years before the Egyptians were ready to think about building something more than practical shelters.

The people who created Egypt's architecture lived in the fierce sunlight of one of the most rigid landscapes in the world: the 1,400-mile-long valley of the Nile River flowing from the borders of Nubia to the Mediterranean Sea. For millions of years the Nile had cut its riverbed deeper and deeper, to flow between steep cliffs. On either side, to the east and west of a narrow fertile valley, stretched lifeless deserts. Each year, for millions of years, the Nile flooded its valley, depositing a new layer of soil on the sun-parched land, and this annual flooding and silting determined the kinds of agriculture the Egyptians could have. Crops must grow quickly after the flooding and be ready for harvesting before they were parched by sun and drought. But agriculture was not all that the Nile determined for the Egyptians; it also shaped their character, their religion, and their arts.

In the narrow valley of the Nile, the only building materials at hand were clay, reeds, and palm-tree logs. Long before recorded history, the Egyptians had learned to make bricks from river clay, which they dried in the sun and put together with mortar. Mortar is a semiliquid mixture of materials that will harden when dry, and Egyptian mortar was a mixture of clay, sand, and water. Good bricks are practically indestructible. Because they are so little affected by the weather, bricks will outlast stone, and with bricks the Egyptians had a durable building material. Unlike other primitive people elsewhere, the Egyptians had almost no experience in building with wood, because trees do not grow well along the Nile, but they did build with reeds and rushes. To make the doorway of a simple house, they lashed the stems of the papyrus plant into bundles that, when stood upright on clay bases, made crude pillars across the tops of which could be laid a palm log. When they did this, the Egyptians were using man's simplest structural principle: that of the post and lintel, whereby a horizontal beam (a lintel)

Two examples of the post-and-lintel principle

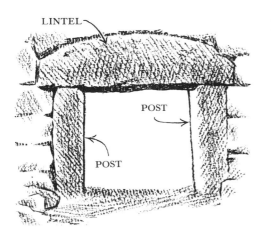
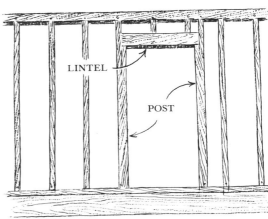

spans the space between two upright supports (posts). The drawing shows how this principle works. It is the same principle carpenters use today when framing a house, and you can demonstrate it for yourself if you will stand two books on end and lay a third across the two uprights.

Like any people who need shelters, the Egyptians built huts and houses and, later, palaces, but their oldest surviving structures have religious connections. Egyptian religion stressed that life, like the Nile flowing endlessly toward the sea, was everlasting. Historians surmise that the Egyptians always believed in a life after death, which was much like life on earth only more comfortable and more elaborate, and that the preservation of the body for this afterlife was an early idea. As far back as 3500 B.C. the Egyptians put much emphasis on funerary customs, and the oldest surviving Egyptian structures are brick tombs, called mastabas, which were built at Abydos for the kings of the First Dynasty.

In prehistoric times, when the Egyptians buried their dead, they placed a body in a square chamber dug in the ground and covered the chamber with poles and reeds, coating the whole with mud. Similarly, a mastaba was built over an underground burial chamber, which often was surrounded by storerooms and other chambers containing offerings to the dead. A royal mastaba was much larger than any of the early crude tombs and was made in the form of a solid rectangle, which might measure as much as 280 feet long, 150 feet wide, and 33 feet high.

By the time the Third Dynasty came to power, about 2800 B.C., the Egyptians had learned to quarry stone from the cliffs along the Nile and the quarries east of Cairo, and with stone as a building material still larger buildings became possible. According to custom, King Zoser selected a site for his future tomb soon after he ascended the throne, and about 2700 B.C. he commissioned the architect Imhotep (who was also a physician) to build a royal tomb at Saqqara, some fifteen miles outside Cairo. Imhotep, who was given a free hand by his royal patron, began Zoser's tomb as a traditional mastaba, built of stone instead of brick. Then he changed his design. The tomb he began as a single mastaba Imhotep completed by setting six mastabas of decreasing size one on top of another, like six great steps, to a height of 200 feet.

Zoser's tomb is the famous Step Pyramid, the forerunner of the great

The Step Pyramid of King Zoser at Saqqara

pyramids of Egypt that rank among man's most impressive achievements. It is the oldest known Egyptian structure built of stone and the first to be built of stone men had cut with metal tools. It is also the oldest structure built according to an architect's plan, and Imhotep is the first known architect in the Western world. Imhotep made no attempt to enclose space within his structure, as primitive man had done with the walls and roof of his crude hut, and the Step Pyramid, like a mastaba, is a solid mass built over an underground burial chamber. It is not a true pyramid, because its top is flat and not pointed, but architecturally and structurally it was a great advance over the rectangular mastabas.

12

Imhotep surrounded the Step Pyramid with a funerary complex—a group of related buildings—which apparently were temples, chapels, storerooms, and courts, and around the whole he erected a white limestone wall, roughly 1,800 feet on the north and south sides and 910 feet on the east and west. Because the Egyptians were then so unaccustomed to masonry—that is, to working with stone and mortar—every block in the Step Pyramid complex and wall was cut to the size and shape of the familiar sun-dried brick, and when beams were needed for stone ceilings, Imhotep had stones cut to imitate palm-tree logs.

With the construction of the Step Pyramid, the status of the Egyptian king, or pharaoh, underwent great change. Until the time of Zoser, the Egyptians had looked upon their rulers as warrior-chiefs, something akin to supermen but still human beings on whom the gods bestowed special favors. After Zoser's pyramid was built, the pharaoh was actually worshiped as a god, a god who walked this earth and to whom the priests of his cult said prayers and made offerings in temples near his future tomb. The Egyptians probably found nothing unusual in this elevation of the pharaoh. They already had many gods and goddesses, often represented by human figures with animal heads, some of which were worshiped widely while others were strictly local deities. As a god, a pharaoh was worshiped as the bringer of good—which to the Egyptians meant the continuation of what they needed most: the annual flood and large crops. And because this kind of "good" would cease if any pharaoh were to die, the Egyptians denied the fact of death for their pharaoh-gods, and the preservation of their bodies became of the utmost importance. So, too, did anything these gods might need to continue life elsewhere, and everything from food to beds and boats was preserved in storerooms and pits near their pyramid tombs.

A pyramid is a simple geometric shape, yet the idea of a pyramid tomb had been centuries in the making. Slowly, after much experiment, the architectural form had emerged, and although the Egyptian pyramids were almost solid masses of masonry serving no other purpose than that of a tomb, the pyramid form of building was developed to fill what the ancient Egyptians considered a vital need.

The Egyptian pyramids were built to last forever, and more than seventy of them have survived, located along the Nile in ten groups between Meydum, some sixty miles south of Cairo, and the Nile delta, where the last group was built about 1800 B.C. All the pyramids were

The Great Pyramid of Cheops at Ghizeh and (immediately behind it) the second oldest pyramid, built for Cheops' son Khafre

built on the west side of the Nile, because the Egyptians believed that in the west was the realm of the dead and also because of practical considerations. Most of the quarries were on the west side of the Nile and there, too, was a rocky plateau that could support the great weight of the pyramids. In places the west bank of the Nile is a sheer precipice, 200 feet high, but the west bank is also indented with valleys that provided natural ramps up which building materials could be moved. And near the site of the pyramids was the edge of cultivated land where the laborers who lived in barracks could find supplies of food and water.

The oldest and most famous of the pyramids are in the group at Ghizeh (now El Gîza), just south of Cairo, and the oldest and largest of these is the Great Pyramid of Cheops (or Khufu), built about a hundred years after the Step Pyramid. Originally the Great Pyramid stood 481 feet high, as tall as a forty-storied skyscraper, but its sides have been chipped and weathered away and its pointed cap has disappeared. So, too, has its coating of polished stone, which some authorities think was made of bands of granite. The base of the Great Pyramid covers thirteen acres, an area large enough to contain eight football fields or the great cathedrals of Milan and Florence, St. Peter's in Rome, and St. Paul's in London. Three of its sides measure 755 feet, but with nothing more scientific than a knotted string, the builders missed in their measurement of the fourth side—by one half inch.

The Great Pyramid is made of limestone, taken from quarries on the west side of the Nile, which was cut into blocks, carefully smoothed, and put together with mortar. Its facing—the coating attached as an outer shell—was made of stone quarried on the east side and rafted across the river. Into the pyramid went an estimated two million three hundred thousand blocks of stone, averaging two and a half tons in weight—a far cry from the brick-size blocks Imhotep used in the Step Pyramid—all of which had to be hauled by human labor up ramps of sand and rubble, which grew ever longer as the pyramid rose in height. By this time, the Egyptians knew enough about astronomy to orient the pyramids accurately—that is, to lay out each side so that it faced a point of the compass. Entrance to the Great Pyramid was on the north side, facing the North Star, in the thirteenth course of masonry— the thirteenth level or layer of blocks from the bottom. From there, a narrow passageway led downward to a burial chamber that had been cut out of the rock beneath the base.

Before this chamber had been completed or much of the pyramid built, the unknown architect changed his plans and enlarged the tomb. An ascending cramped passageway was made and an opening left in the masonry that was known for many years as the "Queen's Chamber." Scholars only recently have realized that this was Cheops' second intended burial chamber. But once again the plans were changed, the pyramid was made still larger, and a third chamber, Cheops' actual burial chamber, was built. To reach this a Grand Gallery had been made, 30 feet high and sloping upward for 154 feet. For the granite ceiling of this gallery, the Egyptians made use of the structural principle of corbeling, whereby the space between two walls was closed with several courses of stone, one course projecting beyond the course below, until the space was short enough to be filled with a single stone. To take some of the weight off the roof of the third burial chamber, the Egyp-

Cut-away elevation of the Great Pyramid

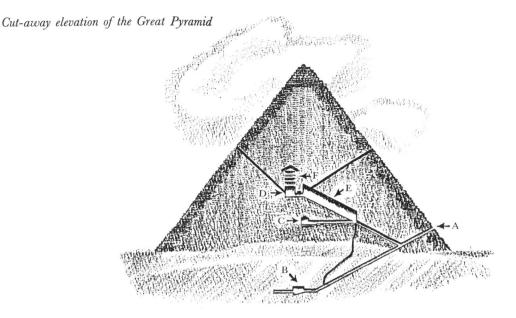

A   Entrance
B   First burial chamber
C   Second burial chamber (previously called the Queen's Chamber)
D   Cheops' burial chamber
E   Grand gallery
F   "Relieving" chambers

tians used a form of post-and-lintel construction to build a succession of five "relieving" chambers. Once Cheops' mummy had been placed in its chamber, the entrance to the Great Pyramid was sealed and hidden behind the stone facing.

None of the three chambers or the Grand Gallery served as a storeroom for things Cheops would need in his eternal life. Instead, the architect designed an elaborate funeral complex that stretched toward

An example of corbeling

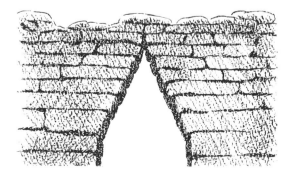

the Nile and became the model for future pyramid complexes. A long paved causeway led from the pyramid and its surrounding chapels and boat pits to a valley temple, near the edge of cultivated land. The valley temple was the entrance to this complex, and there resided the large priesthood (including women priests) that was needed to continue forever the prayers and offerings to Cheops. The pharaohs endowed their pyramids with vast estates, and the cults of certain pharaohs continued so long that when the Romans invaded Egypt in 58 B.C., priests still were conducting rites in valley temples that long before had fallen into ruins.

Many inaccurate things have been said about the building of the pyramids. Herodotus, the Greek traveler and historian who wrote in the fifth century B.C., reported that the Great Pyramid had been built with wooden machines (which never existed) and took twenty years to erect, when actually it took about half that time. Other ancient writers said that a hundred thousand slaves worked on this pyramid while the tyrant pharaoh watched as men were whipped to death or died of thirst. No evidence supported such stories and yet they persisted until very recently. Cheops, historians now know, was an able ruler, who left Egypt in a sound economic position. Egypt had not been at war for many years, so it had no conquered foreign people to enslave, and in Cheops' time Egypt had few other slaves. What Cheops seems to have done was to work out a satisfactory arrangement with his peasant farmers to build the Great Pyramid when the Nile overflowed and farming was at a standstill. Peasant labor did not make the job of building a pyramid any easier, and men did die in the effort. Yet because the pharaoh was a god, it seems highly probable that his subjects were moved by religious zeal to take a hand in building his eternal home. Centuries later deep religious feelings inspired men in medieval Europe to put their best efforts into the building of the great stone Gothic cathedrals described in Chapter 6.

The pyramids of Egypt were one of the Seven Wonders of the ancient world, but the pyramidal form was not widely used elsewhere. It can be found, however, in North America. In Mexico, where the Aztecs had developed a civilization, is the Pyramid of the Sun and a pyramid built by the Toltec Indians, which is sometimes called the largest pyramid in the world. Its base is huge, but its height is only half that of the Great Pyramid. In Central America, the Mayans had developed a

El Castillo, a Mayan chamber at Chichén Itzá

distinctive way of life as early as 500 B.C. They lived in villages, worshiped gods of the sun, rain, soil, and underworld, and had an advanced system of writing that vaguely resembled Egyptian hieroglyphs. Some time before A.D. 900, when for unknown reasons they abandoned their cities, the Mayans built a number of temples. One of these was El Castillo at Chichén Itzá. Its terraces rise to a height of only 75 feet, and its flat top is reached by an exterior flight of stone steps, but it does resemble the Step Pyramid of King Zoser. These three North American structures are solid masses, and each has a flat top that once was crowned with a temple, so none is in the form of a true pyramid.

When the Egyptians came to build temples, they discarded the pyramid form and turned to building with the post-and-lintel system. In the valley temple of the second pyramid at Ghizeh, built by the Pharaoh Khafre (or Chephron) about 2600 B.C., huge stone lintels were held up by square or rectangular granite shafts, which are called piers. (The term "post," when used precisely, refers to a rounded upright.)

These shafts were also monoliths—that is, each had been cut in one piece from a single block of stone. A century later, when the Egyptians were more skilled in stonework, they developed rounded and tapered posts and so gave to the Western world the architectural element called

Colonnade of the Temple of Amon at Luxor, with columns made of drums and topped with lotus bud capitals

the column. Egyptian columns were made in several sections, called drums, and put together with mortar. Because an Egyptian stone column began as an imitation of the old papyrus bundle, it was made to bulge near the bottom where the papyrus stems had been forced outward by the weight of the lintel above. Although a stone column needs no supporting base as the papyrus bundle did, the Egyptians put bases under their stone columns, and when they added a capital, a decorative form at the top of the column, they tried to imitate in stone the flowering heads of the bundled papyrus. At first this was beyond their skills, so they made capitals by carving stone to look like lotus buds or huge inverted bells. In time they were able to carve capitals with palm leaves and other foliage, with the face of the goddess Hathor, and finally with papyrus flowers.

At the time they were developing stone columns and capitals, the Egyptians worked out the essential features of their temples. These were an outer court with some form of gateway, a hypostyle hall, and a sanctuary, with small adjoining rooms for the priests. Around the whole was a wall, similar to that which enclosed a mastaba or pyramid complex. Hypostyle refers to a structure the roof of which rests on pillars. A sanctuary is the most sacred part of a religious structure, in this case the room that housed the statue of the god to whom the temple was dedicated. In Egyptian temples, the statue of the god was not set permanently in place but each day was taken by the priests into the hall or court, even into the city, to receive its morning and evening sacrifices and to hear such weighty matters as legal disputes.

By the time of the New Kingdom (*c.*1580–1085 B.C.), the Egyptians were able to build remarkably well with the post-and-lintel system. For palaces and temples, they developed a one- or two-storied rectangular building, with long colonnades (rows of columns). Although their temples must have given an observer the impression of ponderous stability, Egyptian architects did achieve a harmony—a pleasing arrangement of parts—between their verticals and horizontals. To this period belongs the temple at Luxor that the Pharaoh Amenhotep III (1405–1370 B.C.) dedicated to Amon (or Amun), then the chief Egyptian deity. This temple, which was 850 feet long and had a hypostyle hall, probably was designed by Egypt's second known architect, Amenhotep son of Hapu. Although the temple is now in ruins, many of its stone columns are still standing.

20

Temple of Amon at Luxor

When weight is put directly on a column or post, the post is compressed by the weight it supports and is said to be under the strain of compression. When a beam or lintel is laid from post to post, its top half is compressed by the weight above, but the under half that receives no support from the two posts is under the strain of tension. If the tension caused by the weight above is too great, a wooden beam may only sag in the middle but a stone lintel will snap. Stone is strong in compression (as in columns), but it is weak in tension. The Egyptians, therefore, made their columns huge and set them close together the better to support the great weight of the stone lintels and the flat stone roof above.

Foremost of the New Kingdom temples was the Great Temple at Karnak, also dedicated to Amon, the patron god of Thebes, which was the old capital city on the site of present-day Karnak. Begun by Seti I (1318–1298 B.C.) and enlarged by successive pharaohs up to the days of the Ptolemies (came to power in 323 B.C.), this temple was 1,215 feet long and 376 feet at its greatest width, with two hypostyle halls and a court in front of the sanctuary. As a result of many additions, the design became something of a hodgepodge, and the space that the temple enclosed was cut up into many rooms and courts.

Model of center section of the great hypostyle hall of the Great Temple of Amon at Karnak

The oldest and grandest part of the Great Temple was the great hypostyle hall begun by Seti I and finished by Rameses II some time before 1232 B.C. This hall, measuring 329 feet wide and 170 feet long, once had a total of 134 columns, made with drums and set in sixteen rows. The twelve columns in the two center rows stood 70 feet high, topped with bell capitals, and were 10 feet 7 inches in diameter. On either side were seven rows of shorter columns with lotus-bud capitals.

With its two center rows of taller columns, the great hypostyle hall could not be covered with a single roof, and the flat stone roof over the center columns was at a higher level than the roofs over the columns to either side. When the vertical space between these two levels of roofs was filled in with stone gratings, through which sunlight filtered into the hall below, the Egyptians had developed the clerestory—a wall with windows that rises clear of the roofs below. Long before the Great Temple was built, the Egyptians had invented windows. They made these by cutting holes in the solid walls of their houses

22

and in the holes setting groups of miniature columns between which light could enter. (The Egyptians knew how to make glass, but they did not have window glass.) By piercing their walls, the Egyptians made another important contribution to architecture. A solid wall is not very interesting, but a wall that is made up of solids and voids may be, because of the play of light and shadow across its broken surface. A void is simply a space that contrasts with a nearby solid form.

Big as the great hypostyle hall was, people inside must have had the impression of a dark forest of columns instead of great space. Egyptian architects, therefore, made sure that from the outside the size of the hall would not be underestimated. To give people some basis for comparing size, the columns had bands of decorations and figures, somewhat larger than life-size, that were sculptured in low or bas relief—that is, carved with designs standing out slightly from the surface—and then painted. The paint and most of the bas reliefs disappeared long ago, but you can get some idea of size from the model of the man in the illustration.

No one knows exactly how the Egyptians erected their temples, but certainly they had the help of nothing resembling modern construction machinery. As with the pyramids, they probably made use of ramps laid over sand and bricks, up which they pushed or pulled materials, and they possibly used wooden framework and levers to raise stones into place. The pyramids were built on a rocky plateau, but the architects of temples had to contend with the annual movement of a river site. In summer, when the Nile was at its lowest, the ground was baked dry, but during the flood season seepage from the river could make the ground rise as much as twenty inches. And a site never rose or fell evenly, all in one piece, nor did it rise to the same level year after year. Nonetheless, some of these ancient buildings along the Nile are still standing, although largely in ruin.

In Egypt, tradition became so important that later architects did not even attempt to develop new forms and were content to repeat the old ones over and over. But outside Egypt the Egyptian form of temple was not widely copied even in ancient times. In England, however, there is an example of post-and-lintel building slightly older than the temples at Luxor and Karnak: Stonehenge in Wiltshire. Archaeologists now believe that work on Stonehenge began about 1900 B.C. and that by 1500 B.C.

23

the huge blocks of gray sandstone, called sarsens, were being put in place. These monolithic piers, weighing forty tons each, were quarried some twenty-four miles away and hauled to Stonehenge (probably with the help of wooden rollers), where an estimated fifteen hundred men took ten years to set them in place. Originally the outer ring of stones, 97 1/3 feet in diameter, was made of thirty sarsens topped with a continuous stone lintel. Seventeen of the sarsens still stand, and ten still are capped with lintels. An inner ring was made of bluestone probably pulled on boats from Wales. Scholars guess that Stonehenge once had a wooden rather than a stone roof. The crude stonework suggests that it was done by men more familiar with carpenters' than masons' tools, and the stone lintels are joined in a way that is typical of woodworking.

No one knows why Stonehenge was built. It may have been a burial

Part of the center of Stonehenge in Wiltshire

spot, because bones have been found in some of the fifty-six ritual pits outside the rim of earthwork, and it may have been a temple, because its builders, like the Egyptian priests, knew enough about astronomy to orient Stonehenge toward that point on the horizon where the first sunrise of summer occurs. And no one knows for certain who built Stonehenge. Old theories recently were upset by the discovery of the outline of a dagger carved in several stones. This dagger looks much like one made by the Myceneans, who lived in Greece about 1500 B.C., and scholars are now considering the possibility that some ancient Mycenean, having sailed from the Mediterranean to the British Isles, was the architect of Stonehenge.

The Egyptians began the idea of a grand approach to important buildings (an idea continued by builders in almost every century since, including our own), and they made much of the approaches to their temples. With their love of symmetry—of making what was on the right equal in size, shape, and proportion to what was on the left—they put twin pylons (somewhat like pyramids) on either side of an entrance gate and lined the temple approach with matching rows of sphinxes and huge statues of pharaohs. Sometimes they added a pair of commemorative pillars each in the form of an obelisk, a tall square-cut monolith tapering to a point. The Egyptians invented the obelisk, as they had invented the column. Obelisks usually were set on circular bases and were so designed that their height was ten times their width at the bottom. The great obelisks that have survived are between 68 and 80 feet tall. A pair of obelisks still stand among the ruins of the Great Temple at Karnak and another pair stood at Luxor until one was taken to Paris in 1831. One Egyptian obelisk now stands on the Embankment in London while its twin stands in Central Park in New York City. Both are familiarly called "Cleopatra's Needle."

The idea of a commemorative pillar was adopted by the Romans and later by other Europeans but seldom in the form of an obelisk. In the United States, the best-known "obelisk" is the Washington Monument in Washington, D.C. Built of Maryland marble, it has a 55-foot-square base and rises to a height of 555 feet. Although it almost follows the Egyptian formula for height, this monument to the first President is far too tall to be a monolith. Instead it was built with a hollow interior that houses an elevator and stairway. Robert Mills, the architect who designed the Washington Monument, expected that, like an Egyptian

The Washington Monument in Washington, D.C.

obelisk, it would stand in a large outdoor court. Work was begun in
1848, but by 1855 the money raised by popular subscription had been
spent. The Washington Monument eventually was completed in 1884
after Congress had voted an appropriation, but funds were not available
to build the court.

26

2 *The Classical Greek Style*

In ancient Greece, the highest fortified part of any city that grew up around a hill was called its acropolis. Long ago, a military victory on the acropolis of ancient Athens had been attributed to the intervention of the Greek gods, and in time the Athenians came to consider their acropolis as a sacred place. Homer, before 900 B.C., noted in the *Odyssey* that the ancient fortress-palace had been replaced with shrines to the goddess Athena, and in some other distant time the rocky peak had been leveled into an area 1,000 feet long and 450 feet wide, little larger than the site of the Great Temple at Karnak.

As the fifth century B.C. drew toward its close, the Athenian acropolis was alive with activity as skilled craftsmen worked to complete the last of the new shrines to their patron goddess. In the city below, the people looked up with pride at the already finished Parthenon, the largest of Athena's temples, gleaming in the sunlight. More than a symbol of military victory, more than a product of brilliant Greek mathematics, the Parthenon was a temple worthy of the goddess who was the patron of all the arts and a creation that satisfied Athenian love of beauty. To the people of Athens, this columned marble shrine conveyed a sense of order and such serenity that the desecrations which had brought it into being could almost be forgotten.

When, about 490 B.C., the Persians were preparing to expand their empire westward into Greece, the Persian army was the greatest force in the world and had never known defeat. In deciding to defend themselves and their small city-states, the Greeks knew that they faced probable annihilation, but survival was less important than the ideals in which they believed. When the apparently impossible happened, and the Persians were defeated, the Athenians returned home in 479 B.C. to find their city in ruins. In the next few years, they could have rebuilt the shrines that had been destroyed, but instead they undertook something new and different. The building program they launched surpassed anything the world had ever seen, and the architectural style they perfected has been a model for many people ever since.

On the northern side of the Mediterranean, roughly opposite Egypt, the continent of Europe projects the Balkan peninsula into the sea. The early people who lived there had no equivalent of the Nile River to shape their character and their arts. Instead of a fertile valley and lifeless deserts, the peninsula has many mountains cut by small streams, where the olive tree provided food and a building material, and where in time was found a wealth of marble. For the aboriginal people, mountains had proved less of a barrier to outside influences than Egypt's deserts, and in the course of centuries three, four, possibly five, invasions and migrations of peoples swept down on their peninsula. As a result, the early Greeks were a mixture of peoples, and their character and arts reflected their mixed inheritance.

These early Greeks were adventuresome, and as seafarers many of them sailed the Mediterranean, bringing home information and ideas as well as goods from other countries. The Greeks were no conquerors and empire-builders, and while Egypt under the pharaohs became a united kingdom and, at times, an empire, Greece remained divided into small city-states, whose people had no broad political horizons and united only in times of trouble. Ideas were the prime concern of the Greeks, and to their keen, speculative minds, Western civilization owes mathematics, drama and poetry, sports, and hygiene as well as some systems of philosophy and great advances in the arts.

With their zest for living in this world here and now, the Greeks gave little thought to an afterlife or the building of tombs. Like the Egyptians, they worshiped many gods—a god of the sun, a god of the sea, a goddess of the moon and one of the harvest—all of whom were represented as human beings. Although the Greeks had Zeus, the father of all the gods, they never arrived at the concept of one god, but they did deify virtues and good qualities. Athena, for example, was the goddess of wisdom, and Aphrodite, the goddess of beauty.

Love of beauty, beauty in everything, is evident in what has survived from the civilization that about 1500 B.C. flourished around the cities of Tiryns and Mycenae, the product of those same people who may have been responsible for the daggers at Stonehenge. During the subsequent Greek "Dark Age" (c.1000–c.800 B.C.), this love of beauty was somehow kept alive, to become an all-pervading influence on Greek life and art and religion. It was their ideas about physical beauty that led the Greeks to emphasize good health, strong bodies, games, and sports. After 700 B.C. Greek sculpture portrayed little else than human figures, with the statues of the gods and goddesses representing the ideals of physical beauty. As time went on, the Greeks sought also to beautify their surroundings and their architecture, and much of their success came from efforts to perfect the form of the column.

The Greeks were familiar with the design and construction of Egyptian buildings, but their intellectual and artistic abilities were such that the Greeks may have developed both the column and the post-and-lintel system for themselves. Some architectural signs point to Egyptian influences, but others point to a long native experience of building with wood and to skills passed on from one generation of craftsmen to the next. Whether the Greeks borrowed from Egypt or invented for themselves, they built in a far less ponderous way than the Egyptians. Once they had developed the form of their columns and lintels and achieved the harmony between horizontals and verticals that pleased them, the Egyptians had been content to repeat without change for centuries. Not so the Greeks. Tirelessly they sought to perfect their forms and discover ideal architectural proportions, and their search led them to develop and perfect three orders of architecture.

An order of architecture is a simple building unit made up of a column and an entablature, which for the moment can be defined as an elaborate lintel. In creating three orders of architecture—the Doric, the Ionic, and the Corinthian—the Greeks developed three forms of columns but only two kinds of entablature: one to be used with Doric columns and another with either Ionic or Corinthian columns. The Doric order, which took its name from the Dorian people who (probably) overthrew the people of Mycenae and Tiryns about 1100 B.C., is the oldest, simplest, and heaviest of the three. It is known to have existed in an early form in the ninth century B.C., but four hundred years passed before it neared perfection. The Doric column shaft tapered slightly and at first was rather thick and squatty. In time when it acquired more graceful proportions, its height was roughly four and three-quarters times its diameter where it was thickest. The Doric column did not rest on a base (as did an Egyptian column) and it had a simple capital made in two parts, called the echinus and the abacus. The capitals supported the Doric entablature, which instead of being a solid one-piece lintel was made up of three horizontal parts: architrave, frieze, and cornice. The frieze was divided into two parts: triglyph and metope. The triglyphs suggest that their ancestors were the squared ends of wooden beams, and the metopes the spaces between the beams. The columns of all the Greek orders were made with drums which, unlike Egyptian drums, were put together with stone dowel pins and not with mortar. And unlike Egyptian columns, which were carved with figures in bas relief, Greek column shafts were carved with flutes, simple half-rounded grooves.

The Ionic order, named for the Ionian people of uncertain origin who

A small temple of the Doric order

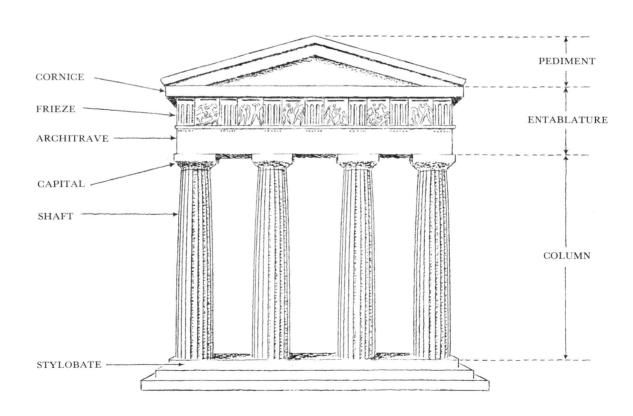

settled in Greece along with the Dorians, was lighter in all its parts than the Doric. An Ionic column, which was always set on a base, sometimes had a height equal to ten times its diameter, and where a Doric column usually had twenty channels of flutes, the Ionic had twenty-four. What really set the Ionic apart was its capital, with an echinus decorated with carved swirls called volutes. The Ionic (and Corinthian) entablature was made up of the same three parts as the Doric entablature, but in place of the frieze it sometimes substituted a decorative molding. One such molding was the egg and dart, and another was called a dentil range. A dentil is one of a set of projecting blocks, and the word has the same root as "dental," which refers to teeth. In the drawing, you can see that a dentil range looks something like the teeth children carve into Hallowe'en pumpkins. When an Ionic entablature had a frieze, the frieze was continuous and not divided into sections as was the Doric.

An Ionic column and entablature   *A Corinthian column and entablature*

Columns of the Propylaea, the gateway to the Athenian acropolis

The Corinthian order was the last of the three to be perfected. Like the other two, its column shaft was fluted; like the Ionic, its columns rested on bases. A Corinthian column, however, was even taller than an Ionic column because its capital was so much longer. The Corinthian echinus was shaped like a huge inverted bell (only vaguely resembling the Egyptian bell capital) on top of which was an abacus. The bell shape was decorated with one or two rows of leaves carved in high relief—that is, carved to stand well out from the surface. One kind of leaf that was popular with Greek sculptors was that of the acanthus, one of a family of prickly herbs found in Greece and other Mediterranean regions. By far the most elaborate of the three orders, the Corinthian first became popular in the third century B.C. in the Greek-influenced kingdoms of Asia Minor, from where it spread to the Greek mainland to supplant the Doric and Ionic.

With three orders of architecture, Greek architects could be far more flexible in their design of buildings than the Egyptians could, because they had more than one set of proportions of vertical to horizontal, two kinds of lintels, and three kinds of columns. But Greek architects never aimed at individuality of design, as modern architects may do; what they sought was the ideal design for a Greek temple.

A Greek temple was a shrine, built only to house the cult statue of one god or goddess. It had no need to provide indoor space for altars and hundreds of worshipers, as in later Christian churches, because pagan religious celebrations took place in the open and sacrifices were made at altars erected outdoors. Whether a Greek temple was oriented in its landscape, as some scholars believe, its site was never selected at random but was a spot that already was sacred to a god. His priesthood was small in number and had no need for courts and halls through which to carry his statue because the cult statue was large and remained permanently in place.

For the Greeks, the ideal temple was a one-room, one-storied building with a rectangular floor plan, and this form seems to have been settled as far back as 1500 B.C., centuries before any order of architecture was developed. At first the rectangular base was long and narrow, but after years of experimenting a proportion of, roughly, 4 to 9 was arrived at for width to length. Since the Greeks were skilled builders in wood before they learned how to work in stone, they probably built their earliest temples of wood. By 700 B.C., however, they were building with the plentiful stone that could be found everywhere on the mainland and the nearby islands.

A typical Greek temple was set on a platform made of three steps, the top step being called a stylobate. (*Stylos* is the Greek word for "pillar" and *batēs* means "one that treads.") Around the outer edge of the stylobate, on all four sides, ran a row of columns, called a peristyle ("about" plus "pillar"), which surrounded a rectangular room, called a cella, where the cult statue was housed. The space between the peristyle and the cella walls was roofed over to cover an ambulatory, a walk that

33

went around the four sides of the cella. "Façade" means the face or front of a building, and a Greek temple might have two façades if both of its narrow ends were treated identically. Each end, however treated, was topped with a low triangular gable called a pediment, with the ridge of the roof running from the peak of one pediment to the peak of the other. As a result, the roof of a Greek temple, instead of being flat as Egyptian roofs were, sloped downward from the ridge to the entablature carried by the column capitals. The roof probably was made of wood or of wood faced with marble tiles. Successive pharaohs might add to the Great Temple at Karnak, but a Greek temple, once it had been built according to a design, was never altered.

Architecture sometimes has been called the "mistress art," and painting and sculpture the "handmaidens" that serve it. The Classical Greeks—those who lived during the great period of Greek civilization— would not have agreed, because for them sculpture was the great art. Greek architects always kept Greek love of sculpture in mind, and a temple provided four opportunities to display sculpture. In the cella stood the cult statue; on the triangular pediments could be placed large-scale figures; high on the exterior cella walls could be a continuous band of high-relief sculpture to be viewed by people walking around the ambulatory; and on the entablature might be low-relief sculpture to be seen from farther away.

Stone for a Greek temple was cut with the utmost skill and fitted precisely without mortar. Instead of ramps, ropes attached to temporary hooks in the steps were used to hoist the upper stones into place. Interestingly, the Greeks seem to have built their temples from the outside in, first setting the columns in place on the stylobate, then raising the lintels, and finally erecting the cella walls. Only after the columns were in place were their flutes carved. External sculpture, such as that on pediments, certainly was painted in several colors, and the entire exterior of some temples may have been painted or enameled.

Just as Greek civilization is the basis for much of our civilization, Classical Greek architecture has affected the whole history of Western architecture. In their own time, Greek forms and proportions were adopted throughout the ancient world as far off as India, and ever since almost every century has seen some sort of Classical revival, some attempt by architects to make use of the elements the Greeks perfected. To under-stand why, one needs to consider Greek history briefly.

Greek civilization began to emerge about 800 B.C. at the end of the "Dark Age" that had followed a significant past. During the next three centuries, the Greeks made such developments in their thinking, their political science, their arts—in all aspects of living—that what is called the Great Age of Greece began about 450 B.C. For architecture and the arts of sculpture, painting, literature, and music, this meant the beginning of the Hellenic Style—"Hellenic" meaning "true Greek"—and a period of supreme achievement that lasted until the death of Alexander the Great in 323 B.C. The period of Classical Greek civilization is brief in comparison with the almost three thousand years of Egyptian civilization. The Great Age of Hellenic art lasted only 125 years and included the Age of Pericles, from about 450 to 404 B.C. If all else had been destroyed, the arts of Athens during Pericles' time were of such quality that Classical Greek influence would remain undiminished.

In a world so often dominated by fear and ignorance and superstition, in which kings and pharaohs were absolute monarchs and whole peoples were carried into slavery, the Greeks stood for justice, for courage, for wisdom and moderation. Among their ideals were truth, beauty, and goodness. The Greeks were interested in people as people. They believed that man was an intelligent human being who was able to control his environment, not simply a pawn of fate, and for them this was proved by the outcome of the Persian Wars. It was then that the Greeks gave to the Western world the concept of human dignity, which hitherto had scarcely existed.

And what has all this to do with architecture? Simply this. Where the Egyptians expressed ideas about life everlasting in their massive pyramids and temples, the Greeks sought to express *ideals* in what they built and, in command of many technical accomplishments, to achieve in stone harmony, grace, and simplicity. Dependent on no grand approach, no series of courts or other related structures, a Greek temple stood alone as a satisfying unity in itself. It was a building with low horizontal steps repeating the horizontal of the ground, a building of structural integrity, where nothing was disguised. The space it contained was neither cramped, as in an Egyptian temple, nor chaotic but organized within the definite limits set by columns and roofline.

More than anything else, the proportions of a Greek temple conveyed the Greek ideal of beauty in simplicity, of a sense of order. Centuries of experiment lay behind the height of a column in relation to the diameter of its shaft, the relationship of verticals of the columns to the horizontals of the stylobate and entablature, of solids to voids, and the slow rise of the pediment. An observer did not need to be in a special mood or to use his imagination to appreciate and be affected by what he saw. The building seemed to be alive with movement—the rhythm of the columns, the play of light and shadow across solid and void—but the movement was contained within the whole. No part dominated another; each contributed to the effect of the whole—serene, poised beauty. This is what people in other centuries have attempted to achieve again when they revived the Greek style of building.

Almost everyone agrees that the finest Greek temple ever built is the Parthenon. When Athens had been largely restored after the ruinous Persian Wars, Pericles, the ruler of the city, turned over to his friend Phidias, the master sculptor and designer, the task of erecting on the acropolis the new temples to Athena. Under Phidias' direction and planning, the Athenians in about forty-five years erected four marble buildings around the huge outdoor statue of Athena, which Phidias is said to have made from the bronze shields of the defeated Persians. The four buildings were the Parthenon (*c.*447–437 B.C.), the Propylaea (437–432 B.C., which was a columned gateway with a picture gallery on one side and a sculpture gallery on the other), the temple of Athena Nike (possibly 427–423 B.C.), and the Erechtheum (begun *c.*438 but built mainly in 409–404 B.C.).

Of the four buildings, only the Parthenon can be called large, measuring 338 by 104 feet. Designed by the architects Ictinus and Callicrates, the Parthenon was the first Greek temple to be built of marble, a stone that hitherto had been reserved mainly for sculpture. The Parthenon was a temple of the Doric order, with seventeen columns along its length and eight along its width, the columns being 34 feet high. Because the Parthenon was both large and important, the general plan of a Greek temple was enlarged to include a second smaller room behind the cella where stood another statue of Athena by Phidias. Both of the Parthenon's pediments were filled with sculpture in the round—sculpture that is not attached to any wall—that on the east façade portraying the scene of the birth of Athena (from the forehead of her father Zeus) and that on the west façade, the contest between Athena and Poseidon, the god of the sea. According to myth, both the goddess and the god claimed the patronage of Athens. Poseidon, asserting his claim, brought down

The Parthenon

his trident on a rock from which sprang a horse, his gift to the Greeks.
From the rock also flowed a spring of salt water. Athena, in her turn,
produced an olive tree and won the contest. Legend holds that later
Erechtheus, an early hero-king, tamed the horse and cultivated the olive
to produce food and the oil the Athenians used for cooking, for lamps,
and to anoint themselves. Along the top of the Parthenon's cella walls
ran a sculptured frieze, more than 500 feet long and 3 1/4 feet high,
with many figures in low relief depicting the great procession that every
four years assembled in the city below to wind slowly up the steep path
to present a new mantle to the goddess on the acropolis. Sculptures in
high relief were used on the metopes of the entablature.

Although the Parthenon is basically a simple building, it was designed
to be seen from a distance by people living in the city below and to be
seen in bright sunlight, which makes parts of the temple cast dark
shadows. For these reasons, while the Parthenon was built according to

fully developed mathematical laws that had been established by the height of the Classical period, the architects made innumerable minute variations to overcome optical illusions. With their great understanding of vision, the Greeks made certain that people would see the mass of the temple as if it were a perfect form. Because they knew that straight lines in certain circumstances *may* look curved, the architects of the Parthenon curved such lines in the opposite direction to make them look straight. Thus, to avoid the appearance of sagging, every horizontal line was curved slightly upward toward the middle. The stylobate on the longer sides rose 4 inches, yet from a distance it appeared to be even along its entire length. The columns and the cella walls were not precisely perpendicular but slanted slightly inward. No two columns were exactly parallel, and those at the corners were thicker and set closer to their neighbors than the columns in the middle, because corner columns seen against the light sky look thinner than columns of the same size seen against the dark wall of the cella. So that the tapered columns would appear adequate for the job of holding up the lintels and the roof, their shafts were given entasis—that is, a slightly curved (convex) profile—to

Temple of Apollo at Bassae, built after the Parthenon but with no allowance for optical distortion

Temple of Athena Nike

a point about one third of their height so that they would not look concave. The subtlety and skill of Greek architects may be judged from the
fact that in the columns of the Parthenon, which are 34 feet tall, 6 feet
3 inches thick at the base and 4 feet 10 inches thick at the top, the
entasis is only 11/16ths of an inch. The flutes of a column became important as something more than decoration. Seen in the sun a smooth
column appears to be flattened but a fluted column looks round.

Whereas the Parthenon is a Doric temple, the small temple of Athena
Nike—Athena as goddess of victory—is in the Ionic order. Only about

18 1/2 feet wide and 27 feet long, it has a front and a rear portico, each with four Ionic columns, and a sculptured frieze around the top, but it has no pediments. The architect Callicrates had been instructed to build a temple on this site about 450 B.C.; although the Athena Nike was not built for another twenty-five years he may well have been its architect.

Although it, too, belongs to the Ionic order, the Erechtheum, the last of the three acropolis temples, is not a typical Greek temple. Mnesicles, the architect, was obliged to try something different because in the case of the Erechtheum he was faced with the untypical problem of designing a building that would enclose Athena's olive tree, Poseidon's salt spring, an ancient shrine to Erechtheus, and a new shrine to Athena. Because the site was so uneven, Mnesicles solved his problem with a temple built on two levels, with a north and a south porch jutting from the familiar rectangular plan. The columns on the façade and the north porch are Ionic, with capitals that are considered among the finest anywhere, but it is the columns on the south porch that have always attracted most attention. Here, in place of fluted shafts, Mnesicles used the figures of six maidens (called caryatids or korai), who carry the entablature on their

Erechtheum, with the Parthenon on the right

Temple of Olympian Zeus, with the Athenian acropolis and the Parthenon in the background

heads with no sign of strain. Built at the end of the Age of Pericles, the Erechtheum has never been surpassed in workmanship. Its north door has been called the most superb in all Greece; the decorative moldings used in place of a frieze combine a variety of patterns without seeming overelaborate; and, although they had been used earlier in the Propylaea, here white marble and black Eleusinian limestone were combined to perfection.

Although the Romans later carried off some things, the four buildings on the acropolis fared reasonably well for several centuries. When Christianity spread, destruction of pagan temples was widely ordered, but those on the Athenian acropolis had been too well built to be razed easily. The Parthenon became a Christian church and then, with the conquest of Greece by the Turks, a Mohammedan mosque. The Turks did tear down Athena Nike, to make way for a gun emplacement, but left the pieces strewn on the ground, so that it was possible to re-erect this little temple in 1835. The Parthenon was less fortunate. During a minor war between the Turks and the Venetians, the Turks stored gunpowder in it. On September 26, 1687, a Venetian shell landed on the temple and the middle of the Parthenon was blown to pieces.

At the time the Parthenon was being built, the Corinthian order was just developing. No example of it is to be found on the acropolis, but in the city below are the remains of the great Temple of Olympian Zeus. Some time before 500 B.C., the Athenians had built the substructure for the steps of a temple that was to be 354 feet long and 157 feet wide. Work stopped there, however, and not until 174 B.C., long after the Age of Pericles, was building resumed according to the original plans. Although much of the Temple of Olympian Zeus was erected at that time, it was not completed until about A.D. 130, when Greece was a part of the Roman Empire. The finished temple had 104 Corinthian columns, 56 1/2 feet tall, with acanthus leaf capitals that are taller than a man.

Alexander the Great became king of Macedonia in 336 B.C., when he was only twenty years old. Under his great leadership, Greece and the Balkan peninsula were quickly united in a semblance of peace and order, and in 334 B.C. Alexander launched his war against Persia. With his conquests Greek influence spread through Asia Minor and foreign influences filtered into Greece. When Alexander died in 323 B.C., the great Hellenic period was ended. The point of view and the subject matter of the arts began to change, to become what is called Hellenistic—Greeklike—rather than remaining truly Greek. Hellenistic sculptors, for example, were interested in realism and in subjects that appealed to the emotions, such as a dying warrior, and not in the gods. Hellenistic architects became absorbed in diversity, individuality, and exceptions to the rules, and no longer tried to perfect ideal forms. This was the time when city planning, which the Greeks had begun in the fifth century B.C., was put into wide practice, when some effort was made to relate several buildings into a harmonious group, and when private houses and palaces received architectural attention. No good examples of Hellenistic domestic architecture have survived, but houses were somewhat like the later Roman ones that have been unearthed at Pompeii.

About the time that work was resumed on the Temple of Olympian Zeus, the rulers of Pergamon in Asia Minor were attempting to make their city a second Athens. One of the buildings erected on the Pergamon

Altar of Zeus from Pergamon, as re-erected in the State Museum at Berlin

acropolis about 180 B.C. was the Altar of Zeus, an open courtyard surrounded by covered colonnades and reached by a long flight of shallow
steps. Instead of being rectangular, the structure was almost square in
plan, measuring 120 feet wide and 112 feet long, and the altar, instead
of being in front, was erected in the interior courtyard. The architect
used Ionic columns, a continuous frieze, and solid walls like those of a
cella, but the general effect of his building was that of a Hellenic temple
turned upside down—the building rested on a stone podium, a platform
some 10 feet high, on which was a 7-foot-high frieze, and above the frieze
were the colonnades, supporting only a simple shallow entablature.
Because the columns no longer served their logical purpose and the
sculptured frieze dominated the design, the structural integrity of a
Hellenistic building was gone. A new concept of space, however, had
come into being. To the observer of a Hellenic temple, space ended at
the flat background of the cella walls. But because the columns were set
widely apart and the altar placed beyond them in an interior courtyard,

43

Federal Hall National Memorial in New York City

the observer of the Altar of Zeus was made aware of depth of space as his eyes were drawn past the columns to the altar.

When Greece and Asia Minor became parts of the Roman Empire, the Romans were greatly influenced by all things Hellenistic, but it is the Classical Greek architecture that has inspired men of other ages. Columns, pediments, and other details of Hellenic architecture are to be found on many buildings in many places, owing largely to the architects of the Renaissance and those of the nineteenth century who "revived" the Greek Classical Style (see Chapter 9). In New York City, the old federal subtreasury has a Doric façade. Now called the Federal Hall National Memorial, it was erected in 1834–1842 on the site of the building where George Washington took the oath of office as first President of the United States. Across the street the front of the New York Stock Exchange has a row of Corinthian columns and a pediment complete with sculptures. In Nashville, Tenn., a full-scale replica of the Parthenon is standing.

To Americans, the Lincoln Memorial in Washington, D.C., perhaps conveys something of the impressions Greek temples made on their observers. Standing serenely on a high terrace, its stylobate, reached by many more than three steps, supports a colonnade of thirty-six Doric columns, representing the thirty-six states that made up the Union at the time of Lincoln's death. Its "cella" houses the great statue of Lincoln executed by the sculptor Daniel Chester French. One hundred and eighty-eight feet long and 118 feet wide, with entrance on the long and not the short side, the Lincoln Memorial does not carry out the 4 to 9 ratio of the ideal Greek temple. It has no pediment, and instead of sloping its roofs are flat, reminiscent of those of an Egyptian hypostyle hall. There are many other differences between the Lincoln Memorial and a Greek temple, but the effect of calm simplicity, the definite silhouette, and the play of light and shadow across its broken surfaces suggest something of the effect the Parthenon must have made before it became "a noble ruin."

The Lincoln Memorial in Washington, D.C.

3   The Roman Contribution

A thousand years after the peak of the Roman Empire, medieval man looked on the Roman ruins scattered throughout Europe and, with his limited knowledge of building techniques, could not believe that anything so large had been built by men. In the twentieth century we are so used to bigness in everything that sheer size does not mean much, yet even today people are impressed by the size of what the Romans built. In ancient times only the Egyptian pyramids contained a greater bulk of masonry.

More often than not, the Romans built for practical purposes—city walls, water supplies, marketplaces, law courts, and the like—but they loved the massive, and, whatever their purpose, the Roman emperors never skimped on what they built. They had many slaves to do the work, and they achieved what they wanted: the effect of grandeur. And the Romans had the engineering skills to build structures that not only were huge but also were so sound that they withstood earthquakes and centuries of weathering. It was man who later destroyed much of what the Romans had built.

By the time of Julius Caesar (100–44 B.C.), a vast empire was being administered from Rome. Where the Greeks had limited their political horizons to the city-state, the Romans looked out on an empire that, in its greatest day, spread from Africa and the eastern end of the Mediterranean across Europe to Scotland. Rome had need to impress the rest of the Western world with its importance, to outshine Athens or Pergamon or Thebes. As the center of a government that ruled over so much territory and so many people, Rome had need for administrative and other public buildings, for housing and amusement places for a sizable population. That was why, from about 50 B.C. onward, each Roman emperor contributed his share of the buildings that made up much of the grandeur of ancient Rome. It is to the Romans that we owe the concept of a national capital.

A capital city called for town planning on a really large scale. The town planning that the Romans worked out for all their cities, large and small, was a neat arrangement of streets, bridges, gardens, courts, and forums (or squares), which may have grown out of the Roman layout of a military camp. Focusing, as Hellenistic architects had done, on groups of buildings and not just a single building, the Romans related several structures to achieve the effect of a vista—a long view along an avenue. Rome was planned as a series of vistas, each of which ended in an important building, which often was a temple to the emperor who had ordered the vista built.

Although the Romans adopted the Greek architectural forms, they had need for many more kinds of buildings than the Greeks had attempted—amphitheaters, racetracks, arenas, huge public baths, five-storied apartment houses, aqueducts—and these called for engineering on a very large scale. But the Romans were equal to the tasks they set for themselves. They had been builders from the distant days when they had lived under the Etruscans. They had no known hillsides of marble, but they did have at hand good local clays for bricks, the dark soft stone of the volcanic regions of their peninsula, and the hard gray limestone of the Appenine Mountains. From this limestone also came the lime they needed for mortar and plaster. Much later, when the Empire flourished, the Romans did draw on the quarries of conquered lands for marble because their own deposits of fine marble had yet to be discovered.

When in the second century B.C. the Roman Republic had expanded eastward with the Macedonian Wars, Roman architecture had been influenced by the Hellenistic versions of post-and-lintel buildings, which were much lighter than the old Roman broad, squat, and top-heavy ones. But it was when the Romans began really to seek elegance in their construction that they turned from the post and lintel to building with the arch. Both the Egyptians and the Greeks had been familiar with this structural system, yet neither had made use of it in buildings. The Egyptians used brick arches to make drains, and in Pergamon

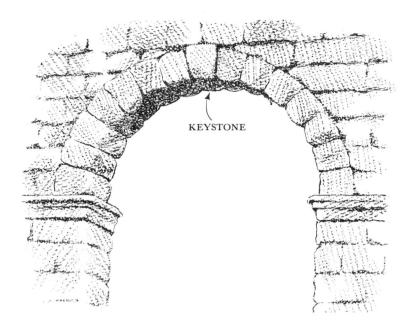

KEYSTONE

A true arch

arches had been used to support an aqueduct, a channel bringing water to the city. The Romans, however, were the first people really to understand the arch, and since they understood it thoroughly they used it in a variety of ways.

When the space between two uprights is spanned with several pieces of material instead of one horizontal lintel, the result is either corbeling or an arch. A true arch is made of several relatively small wedge-shaped pieces, known as voussoirs, that are fitted together over a temporary support at right angles to the curve of the arch until the center voussoir, known as the keystone, is fitted into place. With the keystone in place, the arch is self-supporting.

For the Romans, the arch had two great advantages. Since it could be made with small stones instead of huge blocks, they could use an arch to span an opening many times wider than could be safely spanned with a stone lintel, and in time they thought nothing of arching over an 80-foot opening. Since an arch can support an unbelievable amount of weight, the Romans could build both large and tall structures. All the weight above the crown of an arch acts to force the voussoirs tighter together. This is the strain of compression, which any good building stone can easily stand.

48

For builders—and for the Romans—the arch does have two big disadvantages: it must be made with centering and it must be buttressed. Centering is the technical name for the form (usually made of wood) over which an arch is constructed. Without centering, the voussoirs will fall before the keystone can be dropped in place. Centering can be done in several ways, but it must always correspond precisely with the curve of the intrados, the inside curve of an arch, and it must be made of material that is strong enough to hold the weight of the voussoirs without sagging and distorting the curve. Once the keystone is in place and the mortar has hardened, the centering is removed and can be used again on an adjoining arch.

Since a voussoir is a wedge and acts like a wedge, weight on the crown of an arch tends to drive the keystone downward and the voussoirs to bulge outward along the extrados, the outer curve of an arch. Any arch is subject to lateral thrust or spreading. (You can prove this if you will curve a sheet of paper into a half round and observe what happens when you press on the top of the half round.) To counteract this sideways thrust, arches need to be supported or braced at their weak points by buttresses. The simplest buttress is a wall on either side of an arch —the way the Romans made an arched gateway in a city wall. Another way of buttressing is to build a series of arches of similar size—an arcade—where the thrusts of all the arches are concentrated at a few key points. The flatter (or more rounded) the arch, the greater the thrust; the more pointed the arch, the less the thrust. But it was not until long after the Romans that people built with pointed arches.

The Romans, however, realized that if the weight of all the parts of a building was reduced, the thrust of the arches would be reduced, and it was the Romans who (probably in the second century B.C.) invented concrete, a building material that was lighter than stone. Roman concrete was a mixture of volcanic earth, broken bricks, stones, and lime, which when dry was as hard as stone. Concrete can never be so beautiful as marble, but it can be poured into forms, or molds, of almost any desired shape. As a building material, concrete offers enormous possibilities, and yet, after the fall of Rome, concrete was not used and had to be rediscovered in the eighteenth century.

About 200 B.C., during the wars of the Republic, the Romans began the custom of erecting wooden arches in honor of a victorious general, through which he would lead his captives and his train of booty. In time

49

commemorative arches came to be built of stone, and one of the earliest surviving stone arches is that at Susa in northwestern Italy, erected in the first century B.C. In Rome the oldest arch is the Arch of Titus, dedicated in A.D. 81 by the Senate and the people to the Emperor Titus to commemorate his capture of Jerusalem eleven years earlier. Both are examples of a single arch springing from two large piers that are buttressed by short walls faced with decorative marble. Above the arch and buttressing is a huge masonry block, called an attic, that provided a convenient place for an inscription. Once the masonry for such an arch was complete, all the surfaces could be faced with sculptures and ornamental pillars made of marble.

All told, the Romans erected about a hundred commemorative arches throughout their Empire, some of the later ones being elaborate three-arched structures. In 1889, the architect Stanford White designed a

Arch of the Emperor Augustus at Susa

Washington Arch in New York City

plaster arch in the Roman Style that was erected for New York's cele-
bration of the hundredth anniversary of George Washington's inaugu-
ration as President of the United States. Standing where Fifth Avenue
enters Washington Square, the arch won such popular approval that
during the next three years it was rebuilt as a permanent structure. The
sculptured figures on the north side, showing Washington in war and in
peace, were added in 1916 and 1918, respectively.

51

A section of the Pont du Gard at Nîmes

Monumental arches served no practical purpose. An adequate supply of water, however, was of the utmost importance to the people of Rome and other cities, and in the building of aqueducts the Romans put the arch to work. Once a source of water had been located in the hills nearby, it was no great engineering feat to build an open or a closed concrete duct through which the force of gravity made the water flow. The real engineering test came in figuring out and providing for the proper slope of a long aqueduct—Trajan's aqueduct for Rome, which is still in use, is thirty-five miles long—and in getting over or around some obstruction. The city of Nîmes in the Roman province of Narbon (now southern France) had to draw its water from a source twenty-five miles distant, and between the city and the source flowed the Gard River. To maintain the gravity flow of water and to span the river, the Romans built the Pont du Gard ("*pont*" means "bridge") about A.D. 50. Instead of building a solid masonry wall (which would have dammed up the river and used much more material), they built an openwork structure of three ranges, or tiers, of arches, 160 feet high and about 880 feet long. The lowest range was topped with a roadway that served as a bridge to the city and is still in use. The second and third ranges supported the water channel, which was embedded in the masonry atop the third tier of arches. Because the Pont du Gard was a utilitarian structure, no decoration or marble facing was attached to its stonework.

One of the duties of a Roman emperor was to provide entertainment for the people, which he paid for from his personal treasury. Rome had its native-born population, of course, but Rome under the Empire was a jumble of people from many places—kings who were hostages for their conquered homelands, artists and craftsmen brought from Greece and Asia Minor to work for the Romans, merchants, sailors, mercenary soldiers, and thousands of slaves, the captives from conquered lands. It was vital to the success of the Roman Empire that all these people be housed, fed, and amused. Religious processions, drama, and Olympic games, such as the Greeks had enjoyed, were not of sufficient interest to Rome's cosmopolitan population, and so amusement included horse races, circuses, and bloody battles between gladiators and wild beasts or gladiators and other men.

What is now called the Colosseum was built in Rome as an arena for gladiatorial contests. First called the Flavian Amphitheater because it was constructed (*c.*A.D. 70–*c.*82) during the reigns of all three Flavian emperors, it acquired its more familiar name from its location near the colossal column that then was topped with a statue of the Emperor Nero. The Colosseum, which is a huge oval measuring 620 feet long and 513 feet at its widest, had an oval-shaped arena in its center. (The Latin word "*arena*" means sand, or a sandy place.) Surrounding this were tiers of seats capable of accommodating sixty thousand people. The outside of the Colosseum, which rose to a height of 157 feet, was built in four stages: three tiers of eighty arches, separated by sturdy friezes, and at the top a band of almost solid masonry, which was added later. Into this masonry band were embedded sockets fitted with wooden poles, and from the tops of the poles a huge awning was stretched to protect the spectators from the sun. The whole amphitheater was built of concrete,

53

which had been poured into such necessary shapes as voussoirs for arches, posts, and slabs, and then faced with marble, even to the tops and backs of the seats.

When the Romans took over the Hellenistic Style of architecture, they also took over the three Greek orders, but they used these in quite a different way. Since the Romans built with the arch, they had no need for columns and entablature to hold up parts of a building. The Romans, however, liked columns, and consequently they used the Greek columns and two of their own invention as ornamentation that concealed the functional parts of their buildings. You cannot carve brick and concrete, but you can carve marble into all kinds of sculpture and decoration and attach the marble to concrete as a final coating or facing. The arches of the Colosseum were vital parts in a complicated building system that supported the tiers of seats and the connecting gangways and stairs. The marble columns on either side of the arches were not vital parts in this system; they served no purpose other than decoration. Furthermore, these were not round, free-standing columns but engaged columns—that is, columns carved with rounded fronts and flat backs that could be "engaged" or attached to the walls. (You may already have noticed such engaged columns on the Arch at Susa.) In the Colosseum, on either side

The Colosseum in Rome

of the arches in the first tier, the Roman builders "engaged" Doric columns, or, more precisely, a Roman version of the Doric known as Tuscan. Above, at the second level of arches, they used the Ionic order, and at the third level, the Corinthian. At the fourth level, after every third socket for an awning pole, the later Roman builders used Corinthian pilasters. A pilaster is a long, shallow rectangular pier, with or without a capital, which is attached to a wall. The pilasters at the top of the Colosseum did have capitals, carved in the Corinthian manner, and so are called Corinthian pilasters.

Unfortunately, in later centuries all the way up to the 1700's, Christian builders helped themselves to the marble facing and used the whole Colosseum as though it were a quarry of building materials. A similar fate was in store for many other Roman buildings elsewhere, especially when Christian zeal favored the destruction of pagan temples. Today the Colosseum is a ruin, but enough remains to make anyone aware that it was the model for many modern football stadiums.

Besides gladiatorial contests, circuses, and races, the people of Rome enjoyed a good bath. It has been said that the Romans were cleaner than any other people until modern times because of their habit of bathing daily. This they did at the huge public baths, or *thermae,* which were built for them by the emperors. The peak of the Roman Empire's power and prosperity lasted from A.D. 96 to A.D. 180, and the second of the five good emperors during this period was Trajan (A.D. 98–117). Instead of another colosseum, and especially since he had built Rome a new aqueduct, Trajan decided to build another imperial bath. Trajan was one of the great builders of the world, and he added many buildings to imperial Rome, but his *thermae* was important for a specific architectural reason: the roofing of its great hall was the earliest known example of concrete cross-vaulting.

When a row of arches is put together one behind another, the result is a barrel vault, also called a tunnel vault, which is one way to make a roof or a ceiling. The thrusts of a barrel vault come at the point where the vault meets its supporting walls, and these walls must be thick throughout their length to resist these thrusts. To build long thick walls was no problem for a Roman emperor with innumerable slaves; the problem was how to get light into a building once the thick walls were topped with a barrel vault. This problem the Romans solved by inventing the cross vault. No one knows for certain the name of the

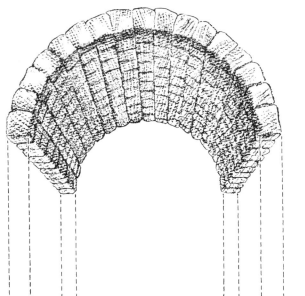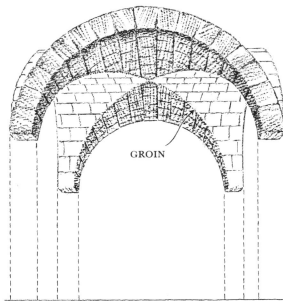

An example of a barrel vault and of a cross vault that is made by two barrel vaults intersecting at right angles

GROIN

man who invented it, but it is sometimes attributed to Apollodorus, the Greek-born architect-engineer from Damascus. The cross vault came into use about A.D. 100 at the time Apollodorus was building Trajan's Baths.

A cross vault is made by intersecting two barrel vaults at right angles to each other. With the cross vault, the Romans could eliminate parts of their walls, because the thrusts of the roof vaults are no longer on the walls but at the four points from which the arches rise. The Romans, however, could not use columns at these four places, because a column resists only vertical pressure, and the thrusts of a cross vault are outward. Hence they supported their cross vaults with huge, buttressed piers. The Romans quickly realized that the main vault along the length of a building or hall could be intersected more than once, and that a hall could be divided into several compartments, each made up of walls or piers and the vault or roof above. Such a unit is called a bay. The Roman bay was always square in plan, because the Romans used only semicircular arches, and if two vaults made with semicircular arches are to intersect, they must be identical in size and height and must rise from the piers set at the four corners of a square. When seen from below, the lines of intersection of a cross vault have distinct edges, called groins, and the vaulting appears to be made in four parts—that is, to be quadripartite. (Centuries later, when the groins received special treatment, a cross vault was also called a groin vault.)

The Romans not only were able to replace parts of their walls with piers when they used the cross vault, but with an arch on four sides of a square they had a place under each arch for windows. Such windows high above the floor made a clerestory through which light could enter the hall. In Roman days, windows were made of translucent sheets of marble or alabaster.

Today all Roman imperial baths are in ruins, and that of Trajan is poorly preserved. We know, however, that what Apollodorus designed served as a model for later *thermae* and that the baths Caracalla built a century later were very similar to Trajan's. Every Roman bath was far more than a place for people to bathe in a choice of hot, warm, or cool pools. The imperial baths were the people's clubs, complete with dressing rooms, gymnasiums, libraries, art galleries and halls to display treasures brought back from foreign campaigns, restaurants, gardens, and covered walks. The whole Baths of Caracalla were laid out on a substructure built up to a height of 20 feet above the street and 1,080 feet square, a much larger area than the whole acropolis of Athens. The central hall was 183 feet long, 79 feet wide from wall to wall, and had ceiling vaults that rose to a height of 108 feet above the floor. One can see from the illustration that the long hall was divided into three square bays, and the clerestory windows are clearly visible in the cross vaults along the sides. The Romans built similar smaller baths in other cities of the Empire. In the United States, the great hall of a Roman bath was copied for—of all things—the waiting room of Union Station in Washington, D.C.

When Trajan came to add his vista to Rome, he had Apollodorus design a new public forum, a combination of marketplace and meeting hall, that was 620 feet long. The plan of the forum was not new and may have grown out of the plan of a Greek temple or a Greek stoa (a colonnaded public building) or even the plan of a city square. In Trajan's Forum, the Romans looked through a triple-arched entrance into an enormous open courtyard, colonnaded on three sides and flanked on the left and right by semicircular wings, which were six stories high and

Reconstruction of the interior of the Baths of Caracalla

housed 150 shops on their ground floors with storerooms above. At the far end of this courtyard was the entrance to a rectangular roofed hall. This was the Basilica Ulpia (Ulpia was Trajan's family name), which served as both a business center and a court of law. Beyond the Basilica Ulpia, on either side of Trajan's commemorative column, was a Latin library and a Greek library, and at the far end was the temple of Trajan, erected after his death by his adopted son Hadrian.

The Romans, among other things, had taken over the Greek gods, giving them Roman names, but despite imperial attempts at religious revivals, the state religion had come to have little meaning. Other people had brought other gods and other forms of worship, including Christianity, to Rome, and with such a variety of religions the general atmosphere was one of skepticism. Much of Roman religion had become a family affair, and in their homes people set aside a room in which to pay honor to dead ancestors and the living head of the family, the *pater familias.* In the public temples, people still participated in the old rituals before altars that now were erected indoors, but the gods were considered as symbols of the forces that made and kept the Empire great and of little comfort to individuals. Since the source of power and order in the Empire was the emperor, a temple might be erected to him while he was living, but this kind of emperor worship was ordinarily quite different from that of the Egyptians, who really believed that their pharaoh was a god.

The temple to Trajan erected in his Forum has disappeared, but it is known to have been designed as a larger version of the Maison Carrée (the Square House), the Roman temple built at Nîmes, France, about 16 B.C. and dedicated to the grandsons of the Emperor Augustus. Although the Romans took over the form of the Greek temple, they did not like the Greek ambulatory and peristyle. Hence when they built the Maison Carrée and other temples, they simply did away with the am-

Maison Carrée at Nîmes

bulatory by moving the cella walls out to the edge of the stylobate. They then ran a peristyle of engaged columns (like those of the Colosseum) around three sides of the cella. The Romans also wanted their city temples to be conspicuous, and so they set them on podiums (like that of the Altar to Zeus at Pergamon), raising them about a half story above the city streets. The Maison Carrée was built this way and so was the temple in Trajan's Forum.

While temples to individual gods and goddesses were erected in Rome and throughout the Empire, the Romans worked out a short cut to worship. In Rome they built a pantheon—a temple to all the gods—where any or all the gods could be honored and called upon to preserve

Interior of the Pantheon in Rome

the Empire. When the original structure burned, Hadrian undertook to build a new pantheon, and it is thought that his architect was Apollodorus, who had remained in Rome after Trajan's death. Whoever he was, the architect was a daring man, and the Pantheon is one of the great Roman marvels. In ancient days its dome was the largest in the world, and today the Pantheon is the best preserved building from antiquity.

A dome is designed by rotating a series of arches around a circular wall. Since the thrust of a dome, like that of a barrel vault, is along its entire rim, the Roman engineers began with a circular wall 20 feet thick. At eight places on the inside surface of this wall they made recesses or niches, in seven of which they later put a statue of a god. The eighth recess was cut all the way through the wall to make the entrance to the circular temple. The dome of the Pantheon was made of brick and concrete poured into molds, and is 142 feet in diameter and, at its center point, 140 feet above the floor. With a height about equal to its diameter, the Romans had a neat proportion of horizontal to vertical, but once again they were left with the problem of letting light into the interior of a building. A clerestory was an impossibility, so their solution this time was a circular hole at the top of the dome. Through this oculus, or eye, 29 feet in diameter, light poured into the interior, to fall at intervals during the day on first one and then another of the statues in the niches. This oculus not only provided the needed light but as a 29-foot "hole" helped to lessen the weight of the great dome. The weight was further reduced by the Romans' use of coffers—indented panels—on the interior surface. These coffers weighed considerably less than solid panels would, and their indentations provided places for the gilded bronze stars that once were a part of the Pantheon's interior decoration. The eighth niche that was the doorway led from the circular interior to the huge exterior portico, measuring 101 feet wide, that had sixteen Corinthian pillars, 59 feet tall, and a pediment devoid of sculpture.

The Pantheon, which has been a Christian church since A.D. 609, has served as the model for several familiar structures elsewhere. Thomas Jefferson was influenced by it when he designed the Rotunda of the University of Virginia (restored by the architect Stanford White after it had burned in 1895) and so was the architect of the Low Library (the present administration building) of Columbia University in New York City.

The former Low Library, Columbia University's administration building, New York City

The Romans carried to a high stage of development not only the dome, the vault, and the arch but also the truss. The truss had come into being in Hellenistic times when stone lintels proved both impractical and unsafe for spanning large openings and when trees could not be found to provide lumber in sufficiently great lengths. A truss is a rigid framework made up of a number of pieces bolted together so that each works to stiffen the whole and resist a specific strain, either tension or compression. A truss is not beautiful, but it does its job efficiently. It can take several shapes, but it is always made up of triangles. (As opposed to a rectangle, which may lean under pressure, a triangle will hold its shape rigidly unless one of its three pieces is broken.) Because the individual pieces are relatively small, a truss is easily assembled on the spot. The Romans used wooden trusses for some of their bridges and to hold up the wooden roofs of such a building as the Basilica Ulpia.

62

The administrative needs of a vast empire had turned Roman architects' attention from religious to public buildings, and Roman engineering achievements had made possible larger buildings, of new materials, than man had dreamed of hitherto. And size meant the enclosure of huge volumes of space, with emphasis on the vertical— something neither the Egyptians nor the Greeks had attempted. The burial chamber in a pyramid and the sanctuary in an Egyptian temple were dark, cramped little rooms. The cella of a Greek temple probably was large enough for little more than the cult statue of the god. But such Roman buildings as the imperial baths, parts of a forum, and the Pantheon put walls around and vaults or domes over

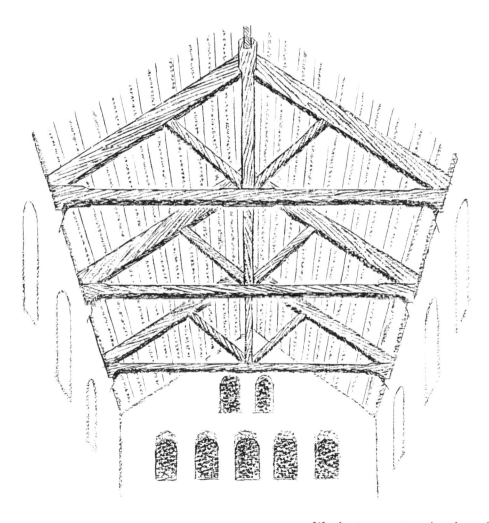

Wooden trusses supporting the roof of a basilica

a very considerable space. Largely because they were able to do this, the Romans shifted the architectural interest from the exterior to the interior of a building. A hypostyle hall and a Greek temple concentrated on their exteriors. Certainly the Greeks emphasized the pediments and the friezes of their temples with some of the finest classical sculpture known to men. Not so the Romans. Temple pediments, like those of the Maison Carrée and the Pantheon, were likely to be bare, while the interiors of baths were sheathed in marbles and the interior of the Pantheon with its star-studded dome was a handsome setting for the gods in their niches. Because of the Roman emphasis on interiors almost a thousand years were to pass before architects again turned their attention to the exteriors of the buildings they designed.

4 Early Christian and Byzantine Architecture

After the middle of the first Christian century, first the Apostle Peter and then the Apostle Paul were to be found in Rome, preaching a new religion and a new morality. The gods of the Roman state religion were the gods of the ruling class, and the words about Jesus that the Apostles and their followers had to say were eagerly received by the poor of Rome. For the thousands of people without hope —slaves, beggars, mercenaries—the doctrine of personal salvation and life after death, of love and good will, had enormous appeal.

From Asia Minor and Greece Christianity had spread rapidly around the Mediterranean, and by the beginning of the second century it was firmly established as one of the religions of the Roman Empire. To the emperors in Rome, Christianity at first was simply another mystery cult that had originated in one of their eastern provinces, and Christians were not persecuted until the worship of Jesus seemed to compete with that of the emperor. Although SS. Peter and Paul were put to death in Rome about A.D. 68 by the Emperor Nero, during the next two centuries Christians were persecuted only sporadically, and there were long periods of toleration during which the laws against their sect were not enforced. Official persecution of Christians in the Roman Empire was as much a political as it was a religious matter. Imperial policy permitted the peoples of the Empire to belong to whatever religious sect they preferred, provided only that they took part in the official rites of worship of the Roman gods and emperors and in this way showed their political allegiance to the Empire. Trouble arose when the Christians refused not only to participate in the rites but to serve in the army or hold public office, both of which required oaths in the names of pagan gods.

In A.D. 180, with the death of the Emperor Marcus Aurelius, the Roman Empire's two centuries of greatness that had begun in the reign of Augustus (27 B.C.–A.D. 14) were ended. Signs of decline were obvious, and periods of civil war occurred when successive emperors were more soldiers than statesmen, often coming to power through military coups. Only at times did a strong ruler appear, and even these emperors were unable to keep peace for long or maintain troops along all the distant borders of the Empire. Barbarian tribes invaded at will, and far provinces were overrun or broke away. Trade declined drastically, and the population of Rome began to dwindle. Eventually, the Emperor Diocletian (284–305) divided the Empire into western and eastern administrative units, and made an eastern capital of the old Greek city of Byzantium on the Bosphorus. All this time the number of Christians in all walks of life continued to increase, and official persecution of the Christians came to an end in the Western Empire in 306 and in the Eastern in 311. The next year the Emperor Constantine was able to defeat the last of the several contenders for imperial power, and a temporary peace was restored.

Constantine is said to have been baptized a Christian on his deathbed. Whether or not this is so, Constantine had shown an interest in Christianity before his power was secure. Christians were so numerous and influential that he needed them on his side, and in 313, in what is called the Edict of Milan, Constantine granted Christians the "free power to follow the religion of their choice." At the same time he excused them from taking part in state religious rites. Although Christianity was not to become the official religion of the Roman Empire until the end of the fourth century, Christians suddenly found themselves allied with the emperor and the wealth and traditions of the Empire.

As one result of the Edict of Milan, the early Christians no longer needed to worship in secrecy in the catacombs, the underground chambers where Christians buried their dead and where they had sometimes fled to escape persecution. But the early Christians, despite their new alliance with the emperor and a growing support from the upper class, were not wealthy. At first they met for worship in private houses or in small public halls, because they could not afford to build churches. Even if they had had the means to do so, they would not have built a temple in the Roman Style. The early Christians had need for churches with sufficient interior space to accommodate a congregation before which the priest celebrated the simple Christian rites, in particular the Eucharist, the sacrament of communion. They also had need for places where the sacrament of baptism could be performed and for places for burial, and the pagan form of temple was unsuitable for all three.

The Romans had organized the interior space of their buildings in two ways: horizontally, as in the great forums, and vertically, as in the Pantheon. When they attempted to combine the two kinds of space, they were not often successful, and the observer was left with the impression of two separate interior spaces instead of a unified whole. What the early Christians did, after nearly two centuries of experiment, was to adapt the old architectural forms to their needs in surprisingly creative ways and to combine the two kinds of space—horizontal and vertical, long hall and dome—in new ways. And because of events in the history of the Roman Empire, they did this in two different places: in the west in Italy and in the east in Byzantium. Two new styles of architecture therefore developed almost simultaneously: the Early Christian and the Byzantine.

Naturally, neither style sprang into being overnight, although the great churches that Constantine began in Rome may seem to belie this. After Constantine died, Rome and western Europe declined, conditions were unsettled, and almost nothing is known about Early Christian architecture of the fourth century. During the fourth and fifth centuries, however, the dogma—that is, the beliefs—and the rites of the Christian church slowly crystallized, and as they did certain architectural features in a church building acquired significance.

In Italy, the Early Christian church developed from the old Roman basilica, which in turn had grown out of the earlier Greek temple and the Egyptian hypostyle hall. The Basilica Ulpia, which was a part of Trajan's Forum, was a long rectangular building. Along its length were four parallel rows of columns that divided the floor space into five aisles, the center aisle being by far the widest. As in a hypostyle hall, the roof above this center aisle was higher than the roofs above the side aisles. The entrances to the Basilica Ulpia were on the long sides of its outer walls, and light for the interior came through the windows of the clerestory.

Interior of the Church of Sant' Apollinare Nuovo in Ravenna

A Roman basilica, then, was little more than a shed enclosing a central aisle and two or four side aisles. Although the central aisle might be as wide as 80 feet, with a trussed wooden roof, a basilica was never a grand building according to Roman standards. But in it the early Christians recognized the hall that they needed for a church congregation and a building that was fairly easy to erect. What they did was to take the basilican form, shift the entrance to one of the short sides, and on the opposite short side build out an apse, a semicircular projection that usually had a vaulted ceiling, as a place for the altar. To frame the apse and separate it from the main body of the church, they built a great arch, called a triumphal arch, which took its form from the earlier free-standing arches that had commemorated Roman

68

military victories. As a result, when a worshiper entered a basilican church, his eyes inevitably were drawn by the rows of columns along the length of the church, through the triumphal arch, to the apse where they focused on the altar, the symbol of the presence of God on earth. Although the Church of Sant' Apollinare Nuovo in Ravenna, Italy, was not built until about A.D. 500 and has fairly elaborate decoration, its plan is typical of the simplest form of Early Christian basilicas. It is divided lengthwise into three aisles, with columns leading the eyes to the triumphal arch and apse.

As the Early Christian basilica developed over the centuries, other architectural features besides the apse and altar acquired symbolic meanings that were important to Christian worshipers. The exterior of a church (usually made of brick) intentionally was kept plain and sober so that it would not detract in any way from the effect of the interior. Inside the church, the wide center aisle took on the name "nave," a word derived from the Latin *navis,* which means ship. During the service, as worshipers filed along the nave in the communion procession, they symbolically "sailed" to and then through the triumphal arch (which now symbolized a spiritual instead of a military victory) into the haven, or heaven, of the apse and into the presence of God. When in certain churches, such as those in Rome where pilgrims gathered, the nave could not hold all the people who came to worship, a wide aisle, called a transept, was built at right angles to the nave. With this addition, the plan of the Early Christian basilica was cruciform—that is, the church was laid out in the shape of a Latin cross—and so symbolized Christ's crucifixion. Unless the site (as that of St. Peter's in Rome) made it impossible, an Early Christian church was oriented on an east-west axis, with the apse at the eastern end. In this way the congregation in the nave faced the altar and the rising sun, reminding people of the Easter morning resurrection of Christ.

To emphasize that the interior of the church was concerned solely with things of the spirit, the only windows often were those in the clerestory, and these might be set so high and so deep in a thick wall that they gave no view of the outside world, not even of the sky. As the light from the Pantheon's oculus had fallen on pagan altars, so the light from the clerestory windows of an Early Christian church fell on those places where symbolic decorations had been placed. Whether it was a wall panel of Christ as the Good Shepherd or a painting of Christ in

69

Glory on the half dome of the apse, people had to raise their eyes heavenward to see it shining in the sunlight. This use of light for emphasis was an important characteristic of Early Christian architecture.

On the eve of the battle of Milvian Bridge, Constantine is reported to have seen a flaming cross in the sky, which he took to be a good omen for his cause. Be that as it may, soon after his victory of A.D. 312, Constantine began building St. John Lateran, the first large Christian church in Rome. In 323 he also began Old St. Peter's as the seat of the Bishop of Rome, who was also the pope. Both St. John Lateran and Old St. Peter's were imperial basilicas, but other churches built on Constantine's orders were quite different in plan. Constantine believed in political absolutism—that is, that sovereignty was concentrated in him and could not be checked by the Roman senate or the people—and for political reasons he took it upon himself to unify the Christian church. During the centuries of persecution beliefs that differed from the orthodox, or accepted, beliefs had grown up, and "heretics" and orthodox Christians bitterly disputed the true teachings of Jesus. To deal with Arianism, the strongest of the heresies, Constantine convened the First Council of Nicaea in 325. This accomplished, and church unity promoted in other ways, he undertook a great building program of Christian churches according to a variety of plans and mostly in the eastern part of his Empire. In the Holy Land, Constantine ordered his architect Zenobius to begin a church on the site of Christ's nativity in Bethlehem and another on the site of His resurrection in Jerusalem. Neither church had much resemblance to the imperial basilicas in Rome, and both are now considerably altered. But because they were built over two such holy places and because they were designed by Zenobius, an important architect, the Church of the Nativity and the Church of the Holy Sepulchre had an influence on the architecture of their day. No fixed architectural style emerged at this time. In comparison with the orderly development of a Greek temple, the adaptation of the basilica was revolutionary, and more years for experiment were needed before the Early Christian Style was developed.

St. John Lateran, Constantine's first church in Rome, was burned in the fourteenth century and completely rebuilt in another style in the seventeenth century. Old St. Peter's became a ruin and finally was torn down in 1605 to make way for the present great basilica. Nevertheless, Old St. Peter's deserves mention because for twelve hundred years it was the largest church in Western Christendom, being 835 feet long overall, and the most important church because of its connection with the papacy. Entrance from the street was into an atrium—an open courtyard surrounded by a roofed arcade that provided space for church offices and the instruction of converts. (Zenobius had designed an atrium to separate the entrance to the Church of the Holy Sepulchre from the crowded streets of Jerusalem.) Beyond the atrium was a vestibule, called a narthex, from which entrance was made into Old St. Peter's five-aisled basilica. Above the side aisles was a triforium—the space between the tops of the nave columns and the clerestory—that ran the length of the 295-foot-long nave. Because Old St. Peter's had to provide standing place for at least forty thousand people, its transept was as long as the

Restoration study of Old St. Peter's Basilica in Rome

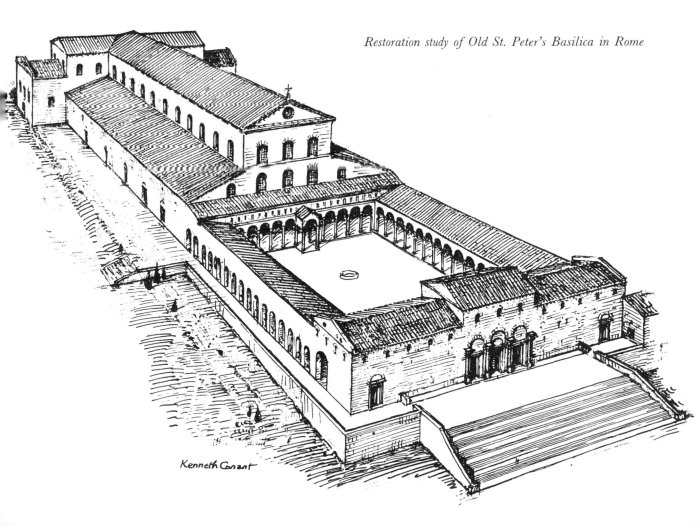

Kenneth Conant

Interior of the Church of Santa Sabina in Rome

nave, but not quite so wide. Like the churches in the Holy Land, Old St. Peter's was a memorial as well as a congregational church, and its apse was built over the site of the tomb traditionally said to be that of St. Peter.

It must be stressed that, with the exception of St. John Lateran, Old St. Peter's, and two later pilgrimage churches in Rome, all Early Christian churches were rather small. Many had relatively simple interiors, unless pagan temples were close at hand to provide marble columns and sheathing. The Colosseum, as mentioned earlier, was a great source of marble supply, and an ancient Roman temple to the goddess Juno provided the Corinthian columns of the nave arcades of the Church of Santa Sabina. Built in Rome in 425, Santa Sabina was not remodeled as were many other Early Christian basilicas and preserves much of its original appearance. Its marble sheathing and mosaics have largely disappeared, and the triforium space, above the arcade and below the clerestory, is now an undecorated band.

72

Interior decorations of Early Christian churches were mostly paintings or mosaics—surface designs made with small cubes of colored stone or glass—the subjects of which were incidents in the life of Christ or other Biblical stories, often told in symbols. Most were done in rich colors, which had a symbolism of their own, and mosaics added much to the interior glow, because each individual piece was able to reflect light, even candlelight. Sculpture was almost never used as decoration, because the early Christians feared they might thus break the Second Commandment and be worshiping "graven images."

In time, the early Christians developed a church based on the Roman basilica, but they turned to other kinds of Roman buildings to fill their needs for more intimate structures. The sacrament of baptism, which until about the tenth century was administered by total immersion, required little more than a sheltered pool. A memorial church, whether built as a mausoleum for an early Christian or over the site of some early martyrdom, had no reason to enclose great space. It was not difficult to find in the small octagonal bathhouses that stood in the gardens of Roman villas a suitable design for a baptistry, and Hadrian's circular tomb and the circular temple to Minerva Medica, both in Rome, suggested the form of the Christian tomb or memorial church. The circle already had become a Christian symbol of immortality, depicted by a serpent biting its tail—a living creature whose end is joined to its beginning.

From the time of the Church of St. John Lateran, a baptistry was almost always to be found near a congregational church. One early surviving example is the octagonal Orthodox Baptistry at Ravenna, built about 458. In Rome, the Church of Santa Costanza was erected in 340 as the tomb of Constantine's daughter Costanza. Its walls of concrete faced with brick were built in two concentric circles, with an entrance through a vestibule. The space between the outer and the inner circle of masonry was roofed over to make an ambulatory and the inner ring, 40 feet in diameter, supported a dome. Also at Ravenna is the small mausoleum of the Empress Galla Placidia, who died about 460, which is the oldest surviving example of a church built in the shape of a Greek cross—a cross with four arms of equal length.

Circle, square, octagon—the plans of these and similar small buildings had one thing in common. Unlike the long horizontal basilican church, focusing attention on the apse, baptistries and memorial churches

Interior of the Orthodox Baptistry in Ravenna

were designed to focus attention on a central point: a baptismal pool, a sarcophagus, or an altar. As a result, a centralized church plan was developed—a plan that is symmetrical about a point. Above the central area, enclosing the space and drawing the eyes upward, was the old Roman dome.

After centuries of experiments, architects had managed to conceal the ways in which they buttressed their domes and to build with much

74

lighter walls than those of the Pantheon. But they still were faced with the problem of balancing a dome over anything but a circle. If a square base were to be used, a triangular hole would be left at each corner. The dome of the Orthodox Baptistry at Ravenna is set on an octagonal base, but the problem remained and only seems to have been solved because interior decoration skillfully conceals the transition from the octagon of the base to the circle of the dome. In the mausoleum of Galla Placidia, however, architects at last hit on the solution. Inside the mausoleum, over the crossing of the equal arms of the Greek-cross plan, the dome rests on four arches and four pendentives. A pendentive is a concave triangle of masonry, much like a triangular slice of a dome, that is bent upward and inward from a corner of the square support of a dome to form a circular base.

Interior of the Mausoleum of Galla Placidia in Ravenna

PENDENTIVES

An example of pendentives

With pendentives, Early Christian architects had solved a problem that had stumped the Romans, but times had become troublesome in the West and building almost ceased. It was left to Byzantium in the next century to perfect the solution.

About the time that he ordered Zenobius to build the churches in the Holy Land, Constantine began the rebuilding of Byzantium into a "second Rome," which became Constantinople (now Istanbul). There he moved his court in 330, dedicating the city to the Virgin and prohibiting all pagan worship. In the wake of the emperor, to work on his vast building program, went the artists and architects not only of Rome but of Greece and Asia Minor. As the capital city of what was to become the Byzantine Empire, Constantinople grew into a center of wealth and trade, religion and art, and although its fortunes eventually declined, it was a leading city until it fell to the Turks in 1453.

The fate of Rome was very different. After the death of Constantine, the pretense of an empire administered from two capitals was abandoned, and left to itself the West Roman Empire sank rapidly. Powerless before the barbarian hordes that roamed through Europe, the Emperor Honorius, in 402, moved his capital from Rome to Ravenna, hoping to find there a natural fortress that could be supplied from the sea by the East Roman Empire. Although the pope remained in Rome, that city was sacked in 410 and 455, and in 476 both Rome and Ravenna fell to Odoacer the German. At that time Rome was said to have been a deserted city, and for centuries after its population was only about five thousand. Odoacer was overthrown by Theodoric, king of the Ostrogoths, who made Ravenna his capital, became an Arian Christian, and set out to rival his Roman predecessors. By that time the East Roman or Byzantine Empire had become strong enough to invade Italy, and soon after the death of Theodoric the old Roman Empire was temporarily reunited under the Emperor Justinian (ruled 527–565).

Like Trajan and Constantine, Justinian was a builder on a grand scale, and even before he had secured his hold on Italy he was erecting buildings at Ravenna as symbols of his claim as ruler. In Constantinople, Justinian was responsible for building several churches, including Sancta Sophia (now Hagia Sophia), which means "Holy Wisdom." Although it was plundered by the crusaders and has long been a Mohammedan mosque, Sancta Sophia remains the finest example of the Byzantine Style of architecture and one of the most important religious structures in the world.

The majestic and unifying effects of a great dome are undeniable, but up to Justinian's time no one had been able to combine a dome with a basilican plan or to build a large domed centralized church. A centralized church seemed to call for a high altar directly beneath the dome, but such a location would interfere with church ritual and would mean that half the worshipers stood behind the altar, which the church could not permit. By the time of Constantine, the original simplicity of the early Christian worship service was beginning to disappear, and in the next two centuries an elaborate ritual grew up, especially in the East. In the Byzantine Empire, every person, from the emperor to the lowliest man, had a fixed place in a rigid religious and social hierarchy—a series of ranks or classes—and ordinary man was well aware of his humble place in a world where spiritual and temporal authority came from above. Orthodox doctrine stressed the wickedness of this world and the joys of the next and put much emphasis on mysticism and the supernatural. Byzantine rites, therefore, called for an impressive and elaborate setting quite different from that of a basilican church in the West. But if a dome was to suggest to humble man the mysteries of the heavens above, a way had to be found to enclose vast space without the massive circular masonry of the Pantheon, and a place had to be found for the high altar other than directly beneath the apex of the dome.

Justinian's architect was Anthemius, a geometer and natural scientist from Tralles in Asia Minor. With the help of Isidore of Miletus and of Justinian himself, Anthemius designed Sancta Sophia as a domed central-plan church, and in doing so he achieved the greatest unbroken floor space in the world. Beginning his floor plan with a central square (over which he intended to erect a dome), Anthemius doubled this area by adding a half square on the eastern and western sides. To the eastern half square he added an apse for the high altar, and to the western one a narthex. In this way he obtained an open area, 100 feet wide and 260 feet long from the narthex to the end of the apse. Along this length, on either side, was the customary side aisle of a basilican church.

To enclose the vast central square, Anthemius built four great stone piers on which he placed the four arches that, with pendentives, support a ribbed dome, 100 feet in diameter, the apex of which is 183 feet 8 inches above the floor. Then to the back side of the eastern and western arches, over the half squares, he fitted half domes, each ending in three cupolas—small round domes. The side aisles were scaled down in height and separated from the nave by colonnades of marble columns supporting a triforium. At Sancta Sophia the triforium space was made into a gallery, which was called a matroneum, because it was used by the women who, in the Byzantine rite, were separated from the men who stood to worship in the nave. Although he was forced to place the altar in the apse and thereby separate the ritual center from the architectural center of the church, Anthemius made such skillful use of Sancta Sophia's half domes and intermediate areas

78

Interior of Sancta Sophia in Istanbul, looking toward the east

that horizontal and vertical spaces merge into one. So successfully was he able to conceal all the supports that cupolas, half domes, and dome make one great canopy which seems to float above the vast nave. From the drum of the dome, the ring of masonry on which the dome sits, forty windows of clear glass pour a halo of light onto the floor below, from where worshipers once looked up to the distant figure of Christ Enthroned in the apex of the dome.

Justinian made unlimited resources available to his architects and assigned ten thousand men to work on Sancta Sophia, so that the great church was completed in the unbelievable time of less than six years and was dedicated on December 27, 537. Because color was so important to the interior decoration, mosaic pictures glowing with gold covered the principal wall spaces as well as the apse. Marble was everywhere—blue, green, purple and black marble, white marble with rose-colored stripes, white marble with black veins, and black marble with white veins. On Justinian's orders, the whole Byzantine world from Italy to Syria was ransacked for marble and columns, and although the columns were "borrowed" from older buildings in other styles, all were crowned with capitals in the new Byzantine Style. Although the dome collapsed in 558 and perhaps again in 567 and portions of it fell during an earthquake in 987, it was rebuilt to its original size. Its mosaic of Christ Enthroned is gone, but almost all the other mosaics now are visible. Covered over in the fifteenth century when Sancta Sophia became a mosque, they have been slowly reappearing as the cleaning, begun in 1934, nears an end.

In Italy, one early Byzantine Style church is San Vitale in Ravenna, which Justinian began in 526 but which was not completed until 547. It is a centralized church, not too different in plan from the earlier Church of Santa Costanza in Rome, but it has an apse flanked by two small chambers that have specific connections with the Byzantine rite. Like Sancta Sophia, San Vitale is famous for its interior and its mosaics, but it is important in the history of architecture for another reason. Its unknown architect designed a circular dome that rests perfectly on an octagonal base because of arched squinches. A squinch is a small vault in the shape of an apse, which when placed across an angle made by two walls fills what would be a hole. San Vitale was built with an outer and an inner wall, and the eight piers of the inner octagon can support the circular dome because of the use of

Interior of the Church of San Vitale in Ravenna

squinches. Centuries later the arched squinches were covered with elaborate decorations made of cardboard. The second tier of arches marks the triforium gallery, which was a matroneum.

San Vitale was Justinian's imperial church in the West Roman Empire, and for that reason it acquired political significance some two hundred years later. In 792, shortly before he became emperor of

Interior of Charlemagne's Chapel at Aachen

Exterior of the apse and cross-ing of the Church of the Arch-angels in Stamford, Conn.

the Holy Roman Empire, Charlemagne began building at Aachen (Aix-la-Chapelle), in what is now West Germany, a palace chapel and mausoleum for himself. To emphasize the continuity of the Roman tradition from imperial Rome through Byzantium to himself, Charlemagne modeled his chapel on San Vitale, and even went so far as to move some of Justinian's columns and capitals to Aachen. Heavier than San Vitale and lacking certain details, Charlemagne's chapel is not a precise copy and properly is said to be in the Carolingian Style, the style of Charlemagne, rather than the Byzantine.

After Justinian's death the Byzantine Style was adapted to civic structures also and continued for centuries as the dominant architectural style in eastern Europe. A church might be large or small and its plan might be that of an equal-armed Greek cross or a Latin cross, but the emphasis was always on rich interior decoration and the central dome, which suggested the hopes and aspirations of man for a heavenly life. Although the plan of Sancta Sophia was never repeated, St. Mark's Cathedral in Venice, built in the eleventh century, was modeled after Justinian's Church of the Apostles in Constantinople, and churches in the Byzantine Style were built by the Normans in Sicily a century later. When it was dedicated in 1959, the Greek Orthodox Church of the Archangels in Stamford, Conn., was the only church in North America built in the authentic eleventh-century Byzantine Style. Its materials are modern, but its exterior resembles that of the Mausoleum of Galla Placidia and its apse with the two adjoining chambers looks much like that of San Vitale. Its dome is set above a square by means of pendentives, and the interior of the dome and the apse are decorated with mosaics in traditional Byzantine designs.

In western Europe the plan of the Early Christian basilica was repeated over and over. The simple exterior of the early churches was to be radically changed, and the basilican plan was to be expanded and varied, yet in every village and monastic church, in every cathedral, the plan would be recognizable for more than a thousand years.

5 The Romanesque Style

When Odoacer the German sacked Rome and Ravenna in 476 and deposed the last of the Roman emperors, Europe began those five centuries of unrest and upheaval that are known as the Dark Ages. Visigoths, Vandals, Huns, Ostrogoths, Franks, Saxons, Jutes—the barbarians swept across the Roman Empire, displacing people and setting up kingdoms of their own. The fall of Rome did not mean, then and there, the end of the Roman Empire in the west. Political control by an emperor was gone, but as a geographical entity the Empire continued into the next century. In one sense the Roman Empire never came to an end, because Roman law, Roman customs, and Roman traditions managed to survive the impact of the conquering barbarians in a weak form.

Briefly Justinian created a semblance of the old Empire when he reconquered Italy, but the Byzantine Empire soon was hard pressed by the rising Moslem power in Asia Minor. By 750 the Moslem Empire extended along the northern coast of Africa and into Spain, where it had overthrown the Visigoths, and tight Moslem control over the Mediterranean choked off Europe's connections with the East. Briefly, too, Charlemagne (742–814) restored some law and order to a large part of western Europe when he put together the Holy Roman Empire, of which he was crowned emperor by the Pope in Rome on Christmas Day, 800. Although the title of Holy Roman Empire was to adhere to a portion of his realm and survive until 1806, once Charlemagne's empire was divided among his three grandsons in 843, the pieces were soon under attack. Again Europe was plunged into a state of chronic

84

warfare, and again the scene was ripe for new invasions. From the east, out of Asia, came the Magyars to overrun central Europe. From the north came the Norsemen or Vikings to gain a foothold on the coastal region of France that today is called Normandy.

Europe was divided into scattered small kingdoms, no larger than a modern county, which bore no resemblance to the city-states of ancient Greece. These were feudal kingdoms, based on an economy of cooperative work and not money, on the protective relationship of a suzerain to his noble vassals, and such kingdoms were ruled by kings or counts, men who were strong enough to defend their rights to the lands they had seized. The people supported themselves by farming, working the lands of the lord who protected them. Towns to support artisans and trade were few, small, and isolated, and had there been goods to exchange, the roads over which they might be taken to market did not exist. People were largely illiterate and superstitious, and life at best was cruel and bestial. In this welter of warfare and destruction, of famine and disease, there was little to encourage the development of a new civilization to replace the vanished heritage from Greece and Rome. And yet, by the year 1000, a new civilization was arising—the beginnings of a Western or European civilization which is our inheritance—and with it came a new style of architecture that was to reach its peak during the next three hundred years.

During the Dark Ages, with no ties of empire to bind them, about all that people had in common was Christianity. Rome had fallen as the capital of an empire, but it had remained as the center of Christianity, and under the direction of Rome Christian missionaries went forth to convert the barbarians and keep the faith alive. In the hands of the church also was almost all learning and all art, and it is largely owing to the monks in monasteries that any inheritance from the past survived.

In early Christian times, hermits occasionally sought a life of contemplation alone in the desert, but in later centuries when men withdrew from a cruel world they sought the community strength and protection of an established monastic order. Living according to the rules of their order, monks shouldered the responsibility for relief of the poor, for the care of the sick, for the preservation of knowledge, and for the education of a few laymen, usually the sons and daughters of kings or wealthy nobles. In these centuries, political power in the small feudal kingdoms changed hands frequently, but men from all walks of life continued to take holy orders and the monasteries endured to give to medieval man about the only sense of continuity he knew. The abbot at the head of a monastery might be a feudal lord as well as a churchman, but whether he was or not, as monasteries grew in size, a medieval abbot was responsible for the welfare of many people. Scores of laymen helped to care for a monastery's fields and flocks, and hundreds of pilgrims made perilous journeys to see the holy relics in a monastery's abbey church. All these and others needed food and lodgings. Bishops in the few towns and abbots in the many monasteries thus became powerful figures in the small feudal kingdoms, and it was they rather than the nobility who were able to undertake such major projects as erecting buildings. And what they built, understandably, were churches.

With Europe in such a chaotic state, it seems unlikely that enough skilled workmen survived to build anything. Yet workmen were found, and a new architectural style began, a style that came to be known as the Romanesque—in the Roman manner. Two centuries before, when Charlemagne had issued orders that henceforth all churches were to be built of stone, men who were used to building in wood could only try to copy known Christian churches from the end of the Roman period. Charlemagne had his own reasons for wanting to see copies of late classical buildings—to establish a visual tie between the Roman Empire and his own—but outside the Holy Roman Empire "building in the Roman manner" meant something else to other people.

In Rome and nearby towns, builders simply helped themselves to pieces of old Roman buildings and put the pieces together to suit their purposes. In northern Italy, in France, and in Spain, however, some of the old Roman building skills had managed to survive, passed down from father to son, and in these regions the first Romanesque churches were built. Surprisingly, the greatest Romanesque achievements came in the northern regions of the old Roman Empire—in Germany, France, and England—where no knowledge survived of how the Romans had built. Accustomed to working with wood, the barbarians had looked on the stone ruins of Roman baths, aqueducts, and city walls with no understanding of Roman skills. Yet by trial and error their descendants arrived at the same structural principles the Romans had used, and mastered the tunnel vault. Having done this, they were able to do away with wooden roofs, which had been such fire hazards, but they came face to face with the old problem of how to let light into the churches they built. In the brilliant sunlight of the Mediterranean regions, lack of light was not important, because a dim, cool church interior was desirable, but in northern Europe churches needed some light. Consequently, the descendants of the barbarians and the Norsemen struggled with their problem until they, too, discovered the cross vault and so were able to build the great Romanesque churches of northern France and England.

The result of three different approaches to "building in the Roman manner" was so many local variations that the Romanesque Style perhaps should be called the Regional Romanesque. About all that the various builders had in common were engineering problems and some architectural details. Otherwise church plans differed; any system of proportions, such as classical architects had used, was missing; building materials were whatever was at hand; and as a result no two Romanesque churches were much alike.

One favorite architectural feature was the tower. Today churches with towers and spires or steeples are so familiar that it is difficult to picture a church without one, but until the Romanesque Style developed towers were not used consistently in church designs. The Greeks had developed a temple pediment as a place for sculpture, and the Early Christian Style had developed the apse as a place for the altar, but medieval builders had no reason to build towers. They simply liked them, and so they used towers, especially on churches in northern Europe. Once they had mastered the round arch, Romanesque builders used arches generously—for portals or doors, for windows, for nave arcades—but they rarely used the simple form of the old Roman arch. Instead they developed combinations of arches, arches within arches, to make a compound form. A third architectural detail found in many Romanesque churches was the wheel window, a large circular window with divisions resembling the spokes of a wheel. (Stained glass windows for religious buildings had come into existence before the tenth century.)

For their earliest churches Romanesque builders adopted the basilican plan of the Early Christian Style, but almost immediately they had to make changes, because a congregational church did not perfectly fill the needs of the monks for their abbey church. The nave of a monastic

87

church was filled with worshipers only on the special holidays when pilgrims came to venerate its relics, but the monks said devotions continuously day and night. Because every monk said daily mass, a small apse only large enough to accommodate one altar and a few clergy was inadequate, and secondary apses with altars began to appear. These might be located on either side of the apse at the end of the side aisles, or they might be on the north and the south at the ends of the transept. Or the apse might be enlarged to make room behind the high altar for a semicircle of tiny chapels with altars, called apsidal chapels. In some churches, as in Germany, a second apse might be added at the western end, and in other churches a second transept with semiapses might be built at the eastern end, providing additional space for the monks to stand when pilgrims filled the nave.

Simultaneously, another change in plan occurred. By the middle of the tenth century a system of musical notation had been developed and Gregorian plainsong was sometimes supplemented by choral responses sung in several parts. When choral services became a part of monastic church ritual some place had to be provided for a choir of singers. In the early days, the monks who made up the choir stood on either side of the eastern end of the nave in a space railed off by *cancelli,* wooden lattice or cross bars. Later, when churches were designed with a special place for the choir between the nave and the altar, the term "chancel" (derived from *cancelli*) was applied to the whole eastern end of the church, including both the choir and the sanctuary of the apse and altar. With additions to the eastern end, there was space in some apses to make an ambulatory, which allowed pilgrims to reach the altars in the apsidal chapels without disturbing the service of the monks. Then on high holidays ceremonial processions could walk around the whole interior of a monastic church, much as the Greeks had walked around the exterior ambulatory of a temple.

As modifications crept into the old basilican plan of a church, interior design began to change too. From the beginning everything about a Romanesque church was bigger and heavier than in an Early Christian church. Windows were few and small, and walls were so thick that builders had no problem of thrust of arches; piers and arches were massive and heavy; and the whole building seemed to express the gloomy, oppressive, superstitious life of the day.

Whether he had inherited the skill or mastered it for himself, the

*Exterior of the apse of the Church of St. Sernin in Toulouse, showing the
apsidal chapels, and with the crossing tower, built in five stages c. 1096*

Romanesque builder used arches everywhere, and one of the first interior changes came when he pierced the triforium, which in most Early Christian churches had been a solid band of masonry, to make "blind" arches. These arches were "blind" because they could not "see" the out-of-doors but instead "looked into" the darkness beneath the shed roof that slanted over the tops of the side aisle vaults. In time, some Romanesque churches were built with three ranges of arches: the nave arcade, the triforium, and the clerestory—reminiscent of a Roman aqueduct or the Colosseum. When the interior was thus divided into three long horizontals, emphasis within the church was shifted to the side walls and away from the apse (as in the Early Christian basilica). When arches were supported by columns instead of piers, neither the shafts nor the capitals of the columns had much resemblance to those of the old Greek orders. Romanesque column shafts often were smooth and painted with Biblical scenes, and Romanesque capitals often were elaborately carved, with figures of devils and other reminders of death among their subjects. Otherwise the interior decoration of a Romanesque church was simple. Instead of paintings and mosaics, a new kind of decoration had been achieved, growing out of a structural element rather than any desire for interior ornamentation.

"Angel of Death Killing the Eldest Son of Pharaoh," the capital of a nave column in the abbey Church of La Madeleine at Vézelay

As was mentioned earlier, Romanesque arches had acquired a compound form, which came about because Romanesque walls and, consequently, Romanesque arches were so thick they had to be treated in a different way than the Romans treated their arches. Whether it was used for a window, a doorway, or in a nave bay, a Romanesque arch was built in so many layers, or rings, that often it was possible to carve or mold the outer rings, and thus better to relate the arch to its supporting piers. This was the first time in the history of architecture that the actual structure of the arch was so treated, and the resulting carvings or moldings were very different from the decorations that the Romans and the Byzantines had applied to their arches. Such structural treatment was a Romanesque innovation that Gothic builders of later centuries were to carry much further.

Where most Early Christian churches had been small in size, Romanesque churches were often huge. Even before the year 1000, the Cluniac order had become the most influential of the Benedictine monks, with hundreds of chapters in western Europe, and its influence on the arts and culture was enormous. Consequently, the great abbey church of the monastic center of Cluny in eastern France, built between 1088 and 1130, became the model for many other monastic churches. Cluny's great church, which was the third to be built at that monastery, extended a total of 615 feet from narthex to the end of the apse. Its nave, which was divided into five aisles, was 118 feet wide and 260 feet long and was divided along its length into eleven bays by great piers and attached columns from which rose arches that were slightly pointed. Across the nave in front of the chancel was a choir screen that shut off the monks' choir and the sanctuary from the view of the worshipers in the nave. But this choir screen was so low that it in no way spoiled the effect of great height made by the ribbed barrel vaulting 98 feet above the nave floor.

Cluny, unfortunately, was destroyed in 1798 near the end of the French Revolution, but the smaller abbey Church of La Madeleine at Vézelay, not far from Cluny, had the third church as its model except for the vaulting. Here, after the nave had been completed, fire destroyed the wooden parts of its roof in 1120, and when La Madeleine's nave was revaulted, instead of a barrel vault, the first groin vault in France was erected. In the illustration, the groins of the cross vaults are not easily seen, but the strong transverse arches, copied from Cluny's ceiling, stand

92

Interior of the nave of the abbey Church of La Madeleine, looking toward the apse

out. They were made by alternating light pink with gray-brown stone voussoirs.

For more than a thousand years, ever since the time of the Pantheon, exteriors of buildings had been relatively plain. Interesting architectural features were concentrated in the interiors, where the eyes of a viewer might be drawn heavenward by a dome or eastward along a columned nave to the apse. In Romanesque times, however, a need was felt for more impressive exteriors to churches. One reason for this new emphasis was

Exterior of the Cathedral of Santa Maria Maggiore in Pisa, begun in 1063, with the famous leaning tower

the great religious procession of monks and laymen that on high holidays formed outside an abbey church to make its entrance through the narthex on the west. The portal leading into the nave thus acquired a new importance and was given elaborate sculptured decoration. For other reasons, arches began to make their appearance on the outside walls of churches—as at Pisa; elaborate brickwork came into use; and towers to be seen from a distance came into being. The first towers of Romanesque churches were built over the crossing—above the place where the transept crosses the nave—as at Cluny or St. Sernin. A wheel window often was to be found above the main western portal, but most were replaced with

94

the later Gothic rose windows, of which they were the forerunners. The façade, the front of the church, also was changed, and the most important façade developments came in northern Europe.

Among the regional Romanesque styles that of the Normans deserves special mention. The Norsemen not only established themselves in France in 911 but in the next century went on to conquer England, southern Italy, and Sicily, and in all four places they proved themselves masters of building as well as of arms. As was mentioned, in Sicily the Norman churches were built in the Byzantine Style. What was developed in Normandy came to be known as the Norman Romanesque Style, which was important for three reasons. It was exported across the English Channel to become the first significant English architecture; it was adapted to the domestic architecture of keeps and castles; and it was the principal forerunner of the Gothic Style that soon was to replace it in northern France.

The Norsemen were, of course, the foremost seafarers in medieval Europe, and in staking out their claim to Normandy they made a fortunate choice. With no roads over which stone could be hauled, builders in southern France and Spain were limited to materials at hand. At Vézelay, capitals of columns and sculptures for the portals were made from the plentiful local limestone and sandstone, both of which were quite suitable for such purposes but very unlike the white and colored marbles that the Romans and Byzantines had used. The Normans, however, had discovered a huge quarry near the Channel port of Caen, and from there they shipped stone to towns along the Seine River and, later, to ports in England. At Caen and at other quarries, schools of workmen grew up, somewhat like the later important medieval guilds, where men who had no inheritance of the old Roman skills learned to cut and dress stone. Were it not for the precise craftsmanship of such men, the huge blocks of stone that went into the northern Romanesque buildings could never have been fitted together accurately with very little mortar.

Inside or out, a Norman Romanesque church used little decoration, but its façade with twin towers gave a new and an important appearance to a Norman church structure. Two years before his invasion of England, William Duke of Normandy began to build at Caen the abbey Church of St. Étienne. (Try to visualize it without the spires, which were a later addition to the tower tops.) Vertically, the façade of St. Étienne is divided by four pilasterlike buttresses into three sections that correspond to the

95

Façade of the abbey Church of St. Etienne at Caen

two side and the center aisles inside the church. Horizontally, the façade is divided again into three sections by a row of three entrance portals and two rows of small windows. The portals, which lead into the three aisles of the nave, are the same height as the nave arcade. The first row

96

of windows is at the level of the triforium, and the second row matches the level of the clerestory. This matching of exterior and interior design was a Norman innovation, and an example of functional honesty, much akin to the ancient structural integrity. The parts and details of St. Étienne do what they are supposed to do (be a door or a window, for example), and nothing pretends to be what it is not (as a blind arch pretends to be an unlighted window).

After the Norman invasion, England entered upon a great building period, its first of architectural significance. In the wake of the Benedictine mission of St. Augustine of Canterbury, who had been sent from Rome by Pope Gregory the Great in 596, Anglo-Saxon building traditions had grown up as churches and monasteries were built. With the Norman Romanesque as the official style of the eleventh century, these traditions for a while were submerged. The Norman Style proved so foreign to English workmen that master builders as well as cut stones had to be imported from across the Channel. Strong Norman influences can be found in the oldest parts of Durham Cathedral, begun in 1093, and at Durham the Normans introduced some interior decoration with an ornament known as the chevron, which looks something like an army sergeant's stripes. This was carved on some column shafts and on some arches and painted red or blue. By 1197, however, when the nave of Peterborough Cathedral was completed, Anglo-Saxon traditions had begun to reappear. At Peterborough, which was a Benedictine abbey church before it was raised to cathedral status in 1541, the great length of the interior is in the Anglo-Saxon rather than the Norman tradition, and so is the division of the nave into three tiers of almost equal height, suggesting a Roman aqueduct. Anglo-Saxon builders liked to repeat a single architectural feature, and at Peterborough it is the narrow bay with relatively slender columns that was repeated. Norman builders varied the design of their columns, and they consistently used shorter and heavier column shafts than those at Peterborough.

The English Romanesque period lasted until about 1190, a time when England's king, Richard the Lionhearted, was off on a crusade. By then trade centers were springing up along the waterways and at the major crossroads in Europe, for roads now were being built and Europeans again were attempting to sail the Mediterranean. Communication among peoples was beginning, towns were starting to grow, and the insularity of the small kingdoms was weakening. The Byzantine Style of the churches

Part of the nave of Durham Cathedral, as seen from the south aisle

Interior of the nave of Peterborough Cathedral, looking toward the apse

Interior of the nave of the Church of St. Front at Périgueux

that the Normans built in Sicily was largely owing to crusaders who had
been inspired by what they had seen in the East. So, too, was St. Front,
a Romanesque church in Périgueux, France, begun about 1120 and
influenced by Justinian's churches in Constantinople.

When William the Conqueror landed in England in 1066, he brought
with him the pieces for a castle that was put together in a single day.
Like other early European castles, this one was entirely of wood, easily
moved and assembled and just as easily burned down. When they were

erected for housing or defense, these early castles often were three stories high, set on a mound known as a motte, and surrounded by an earthen bank. The space between the motte and the earthworks was known as a bailey, and in the bailey local peasants and their cattle took shelter during time of attack.

England is dotted with the remains of hundreds of such motte-and-bailey castles, because between 1066 and 1100 not only William and his sons but many of their barons built castles. Some of the important Norman castles, however, have survived because soon after the Conquest the Normans began to build stone castles. Until the eleventh century, conditions in Europe had not encouraged permanent buildings other than churches. Like their barbarian ancestors, Charlemagne and his successors led nomadic lives, shifting their residences frequently as circumstances dictated. By the time of William the Conqueror, however, the feudal system had resulted in somewhat settled conditions, and king, dukes, and counts were beginning to develop their small realms instead of attempting new conquests and to settle down in permanent "capitals."

The Tower of London is probably the most famous fortress in the world. Its central structure is a castle, called the White Tower, which was begun as a stronghold by William in 1078 to impress England with his power. After later kings had added other buildings and fortifications the whole complex took on the name of the Tower of London. What William built was an almost square structure, a Norman keep, or fortress, that is 98 feet high, 118 feet long, and 107 feet wide, with walls 15 feet thick in places. Built of stone and with only a few narrow windows, the White Tower originally had only two entrances, a main gate wide enough to admit men and horses and a small door big enough for only a single man on foot. Each of its four floors was divided into just two rooms by a wall that runs from the bottom to the top floor. In the basement provisions for men and animals were stored; on the first floor were the kitchen and the stable; on the second floor was the great hall and the chapel; and on the top floor was the king's apartment and his council chamber. At best, the Tower of London was a dark, cold, smelly, unsanitary place, crowded with people at all times. Its glassless windows were little more than slits through which archers could shoot arrows on the enemy below.

As a fortress, a castle had one great disadvantage. Because it was made of stone, it could not be burned; because its walls were thick, they could

Upper stories of the White Tower and other parts of the Tower of London, as seen from the River Thames

not be breached; because it had only one door, the enemy could not easily force the entrance—but the enemy could not be harmed. The windows of a castle were so narrow that archers could shoot only straight ahead, and the enemy, once directly beneath the castle walls, could safely hack away with picks at any corner. In 1154 Henry II destroyed many of England's existing castles, and thereafter a baron who wanted to build a castle had to have the king's permission in writing. As a result, few castles were built during the twelfth century and those that were were bigger and better than before. The lord's keep became a pleasanter place to live when the stables were built elsewhere, and the bailey had the protection of stone instead of wooden walls. Knights returning from the Crusades brought news of eastern castles that had towers from the

102

windows of which archers could aim a crossfire at the enemy below, and so square towers began to appear along the tops of protective walls. Soon square towers were replaced with round towers, as at Conway Castle, one of a chain of fortresses built by Edward I (1272–1307) to secure his conquest of North Wales. Then straight walls gave way to curved walls without a cornerstone that could be picked out easily to bring down the entire wall. One bailey was not enough, and bailey after bailey was added, until some castles were bigger than the towns they protected. After 1450, however, few castles were built in western Europe. Crude though they were, the fifteenth-century cannons could be used against a castle, and no vertical stone wall can stand up to a cannon ball.

Conway Castle, in Caernarvonshire, commanding the estuary of the River Conway

Interior of the choir and apse of the Cathedral of St. John the Divine in New York City

The Romanesque Style had come to an end before North America was discovered, so no true Romanesque church or castle was ever built in the United States. The Cloisters in Fort Tryon Park in New York City, however, includes in its collection whole rooms and cloisters from European Romanesque abbeys that had fallen into ruin. During the nineteenth century, when a revival of the Romanesque Style was popular, people built imitation castles that were never intended to be defended, and the armories in many cities were modeled after keeps, but without a motte and bailey. In New York, the great Cathedral of St. John the Divine, although it is being completed in the Gothic Style, was begun in 1892 as a Romanesque church. Only the apse and choir, built before 1907 when the plans were changed, are Romanesque.

From the days of the Egyptians, people built houses for themselves, but as far as is known domestic structures never took on all the characteristics that made religious and public buildings the great examples of the early architectural styles. Few palaces, villas, or houses have survived from

104

before the year 1000, but during the Romanesque period circumstances became more favorable. A Romanesque house, such as the one shown in the illustration, survived because it was in a relatively secure town.

With the decrease in feudal warfare and the rise of trade and communication, life in general acquired some stability and continuity. Most people still lived in what we would consider squalor and poverty, but more were receiving some kind of education, and the first of Europe's great universities were being founded. Guilds were coming into being in the towns, to set standards for the crafts and secure some social prestige for their members, offering the man who was neither a noble nor a member of the clergy some means of livelihood other than farming for a feudal lord. No center of population north of the Alps was really large enough to be called a city until after 1200, but as the towns began to grow the bishops who presided over urban sees began to rival the rural abbots. The word "see" is derived from the Latin word "*sedes*," meaning

A Romanesque house at Cluny

"seat," and the seat of a bishop is his "*cathedra*," his throne. A *cathedra* belongs in a cathedral in a city, not in a country monastery, and with the rise of cities great cathedrals began to be built. The peak of the Romanesque Style was ending, and the Gothic Style was coming into being.

6   The Gothic Style

Paris, France, at the beginning of the twelfth century was a walled town that in the next two hundred years would grow into a city of a hundred and fifty thousand people. Outside its walls, three miles to the north, was the abbey of St. Denis, the traditional burial place of the kings of France and the repository of the royal regalia used at coronations. When in 1122 the Abbot Suger came to preside over the monastery, St. Denis was a disgrace. Its abbey church and other buildings were in disrepair; its gold and silver altar vessels were in pawn because its finances had been so mismanaged; and the several towns and manors under its care were in a state of chaos. It took Abbot Suger only a short time to restore order and clear the abbey's good name, and it took him only a little longer to rebuild the abbey church. Abbot Suger wanted a church that was richly decorated inside and out, and since he was an important churchman the most experienced craftsmen were at his call. About 1130 he made a tour of inspection to Cluny, but the church that he wanted was no imitation of that abbey's great third church. Abbot Suger believed in the medieval theory that men could arrive at some understanding of the light of God from the light of material objects, and a dark Romanesque church did not fit this theory.

When the façade of St. Denis was dedicated on June 9, 1140, nothing like it was to be seen in France. The three great entrance portals were deep and richly sculptured. The windows were of varying sizes and not evenly spaced in straight rows. The rose window, which filled in what would be the peak of vaulting when the nave was rebuilt, was an innovation, and the crenelated parapet—the low top wall with open spaces—

107

Façade of the abbey Church of St. Denis in Paris

looked like the battlement of a castle. The twin towers (the north one
has been destroyed) and the verticals of the four great buttresses suggested the master mason's familiarity with William the Conqueror's
church at Caen, but the austere effect of St. Étienne was missing. At St.
Denis all was combined to pull the eyes of the beholder upward to the
tower spires rising toward God.

One month after the façade was dedicated, Abbot Suger had his men
at work rebuilding the apse, which customarily was the first part of a
church to be completed. In the amazingly short space of three years and
three months, the apse was finished and on June 11, 1144, it was dedicated with nineteen bishops simultaneously saying a Mass of Masses
before nineteen gilded altars.

If St. Denis's façade was a departure from the Romanesque, its apse was a revolutionary conception. Gone was the simple semicircle of the Early Christian or Romanesque apse, and in its place was an elongated apse that from the outside looked like a series of stone scallops, quite different in appearance even from the apse of St. Sernin. In France, an apse in this shape came to be called a chevet. At St. Denis the outer wall had been so cut away that little more than buttresses remained to frame the fourteen stained glass windows. Inside were two ambulatories instead of one, separated by only a semicircular row of eight columns. Rimming the outer ambulatory were seven shallow arc-shaped apsidal chapels, which accounted for the exterior scallops. Each chapel was framed with a pointed arch, and in each was a pair of stained glass windows. In those days stained glass was looked upon as a mystery because it glowed without fire. Stained glass also had the richness of jewels, and when the warm glow from the chapel windows fell across the ambulatories to light the interior and touch the vessels on the altar, even Abbot Suger was satisfied.

St. Denis was the first building in the Gothic Style, but the name "Gothic," like "Romanesque" and other such names, of course was not used by those who practiced the style. Sixteenth-century Italians were impressed with all things classic—with Greek and Roman culture—and since the pointed arch was not classic, it was considered barbaric, even "Gothic," the ultimate word of contempt in those days. But no contempt was felt in the twelfth century—or today. St. Denis inspired other bishops to start building cathedrals, and the new building system spread rapidly throughout Europe to become the only way of building (except in Italy) until well into the sixteenth century.

Unlike the Early Christian and the Romanesque styles, the Gothic did not come into being to fill a new need. The aisled plan of an Early Christian church, with or without a transept, was still essential. Although a cathedral nave was likely to be longer than that of a monastic church, in order to accommodate many worshipers, the liturgical needs of the twelfth-century church had not suddenly changed, and a nave, a choir, places for minor altars, and enough room for processions were required in a city cathedral as much as in an abbey church. The three architectural features that are characteristic of the Gothic Style—the pointed arch, the ribbed vault, and the flying buttress—had been used by Romanesque builders, but all three had never been used together in any one building. Beginning at St. Denis, the Gothic Style emerged as master masons, who

Interior of the chevet of St. Denis

were both engineers and artists, saw the aesthetic possibilities of the three features and combined them into a unified structural system that made possible sound tall buildings and an effect of great lightness. Much as the Greek temple had evolved centuries before, the Gothic developed logically out of the structural soundness of the Romanesque and the aesthetic possibilities it suggested.

Whoever he was—and in all that Abbot Suger wrote about the building of St. Denis his name is not mentioned—the master builder of St. Denis had discovered that with a pointed arch he had a graceful form for his ambulatory arcades and chapel frames and the means with which to vault the irregularly shaped bays of his chevet. The chevet was divided by columns into two sets of irregularly shaped bays, neither of which a Romanesque builder with his semicircular arch would have attempted to vault. If semicircular arches of the same height are to intersect, they must start from the corners of a square bay. The builder of St. Denis, however, realized that pointed arches will intersect when those on the short sides of a rectangular or irregularly shaped bay are pointed steeply and those on the long sides are pointed gently. For aesthetic reasons and as extra support, he added a fifth rib in each vault over the outer ambulatory. Gothic pointed arched ribs are often referred to as ogives.

A groin vault, such as that at La Madeleine, had to be made with heavy stones, but the shorter spaces between ribs at St. Denis could be filled with a web of thin small stones, which lightened the weight of the vault. When the outer wall supported less weight, the builder could cut parts of it away to make space for his windows. With pointed arches and more than four ribs, Gothic vaulting soon began to rise in height, and when the flying buttress was perfected, clerestory and vaults could rise still higher and more and more of the walls could be replaced with more and larger windows.

The original buttresses of the chevet of St. Denis were not flying buttresses, although flying buttresses had been used both at Cluny and at Durham, hidden from sight under the roofs over the side aisles. Not long after it had been completed, the nave vaulting of Cluny's third church fell in parts. A height of 98 feet had gone beyond Romanesque knowledge of engineering, and out of this accident seems to have come the discovery of the flying buttress. Cluny, naturally, could not be left with an unvaulted nave, and when the vaulting was again attempted, the builders supported it in places on the outside with a range of open round arches "flying" up from strategic spots to push against the points of thrust. Most authorities hold that the first Gothic flying buttresses that were parts of a structural plan and not afterthoughts were developed about 1180 at the Cathedral of Notre Dame in Paris.

In themselves, the pointed arch, ribbed vault, and flying buttress do not make up the Gothic Style. They are simply the characteristic

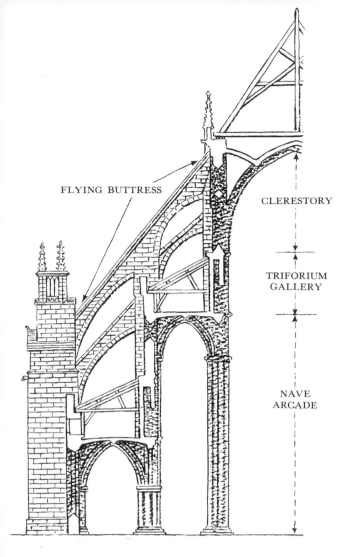

FLYING BUTTRESS

CLERESTORY

TRIFORIUM
GALLERY

NAVE
ARCADE

A flying buttress of Bourges Cathedral

features. Gothic builders were very much aware of space, and in the soaring cathedrals they built they were trying to enclose space in ways that would express the philosophy and the spirit of the day. Europe in the twelfth and thirteenth centuries witnessed a religious enthusiasm that has never again been matched. Hardly had the chevet of St. Denis been dedicated when the bishops of Sens, Senlis, Laon, Noyon, and Paris were planning cathedrals of their own. The earliest Gothic cathedrals were built in the Île de France, a fluctuating but roughly circular area radiating a hundred miles from Paris, that the kings of France claimed as their royal territory. France then was only a small kingdom, and yet during the twelfth and thirteenth centuries eighty Gothic cathedrals and five hundred large Gothic churches were built there.

With St. Denis pointing the way, medieval builders began to experiment with lofty, well-lighted cathedrals in which height would not be attained at the expense of stability. One of the earliest developments was the vault with six ribs, which was worked out at Sens (begun 1145). With the support of two extra ribs, the weight of the vault became less of a problem, and the stone boss, or nob, formed where the six ribs met suggested a new kind of ceiling decoration. A second experiment at Sens involved the use of colonettes at all levels of the nave. In time colonettes—slender half columns attached to the wall—became important features of Gothic interiors, because they helped to channel some of the pressures of the vault to the nave columns far below.

Interior of the nave of Sens Cathedral, with its six-part vaults and blind arches of the triforium passageway

Although the arches now were pointed, the great nave colonnade remained much as it had been in a Romanesque church. The columns, usually made in drums, still had to carry the weight of all that was built above. It was the second level of the nave, the triforium, where the most important early Gothic developments occurred. What in a Romanesque church had been a row of blind arches now became a passageway above the side aisle, and the wall, which formerly had been a solid support, became two thin walls, one on either side of the passage. When the inner wall was made into an arcade (as at Laon, begun in 1160), this thin wall was further cut away, but the arches also helped to split up and support the pressures from above. In later Gothic cathedrals, however, the triforium seldom had outside windows, and consequently when seen from inside it appeared as a dark band between the nave and the clerestory, both of which were lighted by windows.

At Laon and Noyon (also begun in 1160) builders experimented with a fourth story in their efforts to achieve height. In both these cathedrals, the fourth story took the form of a band of blind arches between the triforium and the clerestory. At the Cathedral of Notre Dame in Paris (begun 1163), however, the fourth story was a row of roses—not rose windows but glassless round openings—the circular frames of which acted like arches and strengthened the wall at this height.

Sens was a large cathedral, but it was not a lofty one. Cluny had been 98 feet high. Sens and Laon were only 79 feet high, but the builder of Notre Dame decided to risk a height of 107 feet for his nave vaulting. As he cut away piece after piece of the upper walls for windows, he knew that the time had come to shore up the walls in some fashion, so he made use of the flying buttress to do the job. Notre Dame is considered the last of the early Gothic cathedrals, and thereafter, with the flying buttress put to work, builders discarded a fourth story as a way to gain height. With this exterior support, a fourth tier of arches to help in distributing the thrusts of the vaults was no longer needed, and Gothic vaults rose higher and higher and windows became longer and longer.

As the nave vaulting gained in height, so too did the clerestory. Lancet windows—tall narrow windows with pointed tops and undecorated openings—had appeared on the façade of St. Denis. Now as the

Interior of the nave of Laon Cathedral

number and size of the windows of a Gothic cathedral grew, taller and taller lancet windows were used to add height to the clerestory. Rose windows also grew in size and in use, and were to be found above the portals at the ends of the transept as well as on the west façade. The rose window was so named because of the resemblance to a rose that is created by the intricately carved stonework, called tracery, which fills its circular area. This tracery not only provided a grill into which small pieces of stained glass could be fitted but also acted as resistance to the wind pressure that might otherwise have blown out the glass.

Cathedral of Notre Dame in Paris, as seen from the River Seine

On the outside, a Gothic cathedral looks very different from a Romanesque one. The exterior of any Gothic cathedral was governed by what was done to the interior, and all the effort that went to achieve a soaring well-lighted interior, on the outside resulted in many windows, pointed arches, and (especially in France) flying buttresses. In addition, sculpture could be found almost everywhere on the outside of a Gothic church. Since transepts, whether long or short, had been retained, their façades received almost as elaborate treatment as the main western façade, and as the portals of the façades grew deeper, more rings of masonry were available for carving. It is possible to find as many as seven hundred individual figures carved into the portals of only one façade of some cathedrals. This is one reason that Gothic cathedrals have been called "the Bible in stone and glass," because almost every Bible story was carved there for the people to "read." Other sculptures preserved history, philosophy, and natural history in stone, while much information about the customs of the times is to be gained from the stained glass windows that were the gifts of the guilds. Among the sculptured saints and angels gargoyles can sometimes be found. Some of these were decorations symbolizing demons fleeing from a sacred building, but other gargoyles function as waterspouts. The wooden roofs that kept the rain and snow from reaching the stone vaulting of the nave had no gutters, and waterspouts were necessary.

One of the gargoyles of the Cathedral of Notre Dame in Paris

Once a bishop had approved the plans for his Gothic cathedral, a site was cleared and the foundation crowded in among the surrounding buildings. No one paid much attention to the setting of a cathedral, but Gothic builders were very much aware of its skyline. The builder of Laon, besides the two towers of the west façade, had raised a tower at each end of the transept and, in addition, built over the crossing a very slender tower, called a flèche (meaning "arrow"), so that Laon had five towers. Many later Gothic cathedrals omitted tower spires, but in France almost every cathedral had a flèche like that of Notre Dame. When the Gothic Style spread to England, neither the flying buttress nor the flèche became popular, and English Gothic cathedrals, such as Salisbury Cathedral, retained the substantial crossing tower of the past. Perhaps this was because English cathedrals were not so high as French ones and were built in more rural settings, not surrounded by city houses as in France, and hence seemed to have less need for such features to dominate their surroundings.

Whatever its setting, a cathedral was the center of town life, while the bell that pealed forth from its tower regulated the lives of all in the surrounding countryside. Likely as not, a cathedral was surrounded by other church buildings, such as a bishop's palace, a cloister, an almshouse, and a school dedicated to the Virgin as patron of all the arts. In France, narrow streets fanned out from the cathedral square, and on these streets were both shops and houses. According to the custom of that day, the men who followed a specific craft lived on the same street, so a city had one street for its bakers, another for its masons, and so on through the trades. At times the portals of a cathedral served as the backdrop for a religious play or the performance of traveling jugglers and minstrels; at other times, the nave doubled as a town hall.

A Gothic cathedral was the greatest product that a town's craftsmen could make, and into it went the finest work of stone cutters, masons, carpenters, stained glass and metal workers, those who made the candles and the communion bread, and countless others. In the thirteenth and fourteenth centuries, what had been developed in the twelfth century was carried to perfection—and sometimes beyond. At Chartres (begun 1194) and Amiens (begun 1220), the six-rib vault, the colonette, and the pointed arch combined to make a unified whole, where emphasis no longer was on the walls or the ceiling but on all interior

Exterior of Salisbury Cathedral, as seen from the southwest

parts that were flooded with light. The nave was still divided into three
horizontals as in Romanesque times, but the horizontal effect was offset by the upward pull of so many verticals. No longer were the eyes
of the worshiper focused immediately on the apse. Instead, his eyes
were drawn slowly eastward by a combination of many parts into a
spatial relationship far more subtle than in any earlier architecture.
From pillar to arch, from colonette to vault, from arch to arch, from
window to window—everywhere was an effect of continuous movement.

The cathedrals of Amiens, Chartres, and Rheims (begun 1211) in
France all are famous for their exterior sculptures, but revolution and

Interior of the nave of Chartres Cathedral

wars were not kind to French cathedrals, and only Chartres retains its original stained glass. Like Notre Dame of Paris, St. Denis had its nave rebuilt in the thirteenth century and was mutilated during the French Revolution.

Since a cathedral was the pride and joy of its people, civic rivalry led to higher and higher cathedrals. Chartres rose 122 feet; Rheims and Bourges (begun 1192) were a little higher. Amiens, which is the largest cathedral in France, enclosing 784,800 cubic feet of space, went to 147 feet, and then Beauvais (begun 1247) rose to 157. These additional 10 feet did not mean a new structural development; they meant only that Beauvais had gone beyond the Gothic limit. In 1284 half the nave vaulting fell, and to this day Beauvais remains an unfinished cathedral.

In England, Gothic builders never strove for height, but English cathedrals were bigger and wider, if lower, than those in France. England retained the older simple apse and seldom used the flying buttress, though Salisbury Cathedral is among the few exceptions. English cathedrals, therefore, do not have chevets, although they do have apsidal chapels. In both English and French cathedrals, the main chapel behind the altar is known as the Lady Chapel, dedicated to the Virgin Mary.

In later centuries, as Gothic builders divided their vaults with more and more ribs, too many ribs created problems, just as too much height did. Many ribs crossing at one point made complications. At Exeter Cathedral (begun c.1280), each vault has sixteen ribs springing from colonettes no thicker than a reed, but the ribs still work at supporting the vault. By the time (1500–1512) Henry VII added his chapel to Westminster Abbey, many of the ribs had become simply ceiling decorations. So many ribs were involved that the bosses had become great stone pendants, and the ceiling looks more like lace than a stone rib vault.

Gothic cathedrals were huge structures and rich with decorations, but, contrary to general belief, they did not take centuries to build. Some cathedrals, of course, were not finished in the same century in which their cornerstones were laid, but the actual building time was surprisingly short. Although its belfries and some other details were added much later, Chartres Cathedral was built in the twenty-seven

Interior of the Henry VII Chapel in Westminster Abbey, London

years between 1194 and 1221. (The north tower, on the left, 377 feet high, was finished in 1513.) If the original funds ran out, some cathedrals were built in two stages. Bourges Cathedral was built during 1192–1214 and 1225–*c*.1255, but the work here and in similar instances was so organized that the parts begun were carried to completion and put into use before work had to cease.

As in earlier times, the church was the great builder during the Gothic period. If a bishop wanted a cathedral, he helped with the plans, secured their approval, undertook to raise the funds, and administered the project, but the man responsible for the construction

Façade of Chartres Cathedral

of a Gothic cathedral was a master builder. He might be called the master mason, master stonecutter, or master cementer, but whatever his title he was the equivalent of a modern architect, engineer, contractor, and subcontractor rolled into one. Everything that went into a cathedral was his responsibility—from substructure to sculptures, stained glass, and furnishings—and had his on-the-spot supervision. He knew nothing about that branch of descriptive geometry that architects use today, but he did know how to make three-dimensional models, and he was far more accomplished than his Romanesque equivalent. Although anonymity was the prescribed order of the day, and men worked for a cause and not their own fame, the names of some of the men who built the Gothic cathedrals are known. Known or unknown, these master builders were also artists, and their accomplishments were so respected that their successors rarely changed what they had built.

Unlike a modern builder, the Gothic master mason had no way to calculate statics—the weight of material at rest—but he worked with only one material: stone. Stone is trustworthy only in its resistance to compression, but medieval builders came to know everything there was to know about working in stone, and their solutions of the structural problems posed by this building material have never since been equaled, let alone surpassed. For one reason, men in the Gothic time worked only with hand tools and, stroke by stroke, they were able to observe the quality or the flaws of each individual stone.

Once its lower course of stone had been laid, a Gothic cathedral rose through the ingenious use of scaffolding. Scaffolding might be set into temporary holes in the permanent masonry, and then dismantled when what had been built became the solid base for new scaffolding for still higher construction. Architecturally, the triforium gallery served to lighten a cathedral's walls, but while a cathedral was being built the triforium passages were another kind of scaffolding. So, too, were the galleries at the clerestory level, either inside or out, and the exterior walks that are found behind the parapet at the edge of the nave roof or the side aisle roofs in almost every Gothic cathedral. Medieval scaffolding was for the use of workmen only, and large blocks of stone were lifted from inside the cathedral to the point of construction by crude cranes and derricks, which might rest on a finished wall. Other materials were loaded on barrows and pushed along

*"Building of the Temple of Jerusalem." Although Jean Fouquet (c.1415–1480)
painted the original of this scene as an illustration for a translation of Josephus'*
ANTIQUITES JUDAIQUES, *he actually depicted the construction of a late Gothic
cathedral in his native France*

the walls, and workmen could carry hods up the little spiral staircases that are fitted into corners or concealed inside buttresses in most cathedrals. Once a cathedral was completed, the galleries and the walks behind the parapets connected those parts that were on the same level and made it possible to repair the masonry or windows high above the ground.

As a section of a cathedral was being built, all work was completed to a specific level before any higher work was attempted. As he planned his cathedral, the master builder had to determine in advance the supports for his vaulting. When he was ready to build a vault, he laid out on the floor of his workshop the curve he had worked out for the ribs and then cut each stone voussoir to fit into its place on the curve. But before this was done, the walls had been built to the desired height, and the flying buttresses were in place, waiting to carry the thrusts the vaults would exert.

It has been said that Gothic builders shaped stones so perfectly that their arches would have stood without the mortar that was used, and this is probably true. Gothic builders used mortar only to reinforce stone joints, and French Gothic mortar, made with a "fat" or "aerated" lime, took a long time to set. Experts have estimated that where walls were thick and mortar not exposed to air, the drying time was over a century. It seems possible that in later Gothic churches the naves were temporarily roofed with wood and the vaulting not attempted until the mortar in the lower walls had been given a year or more to harden. Any structure made of stone takes years to settle, and no Gothic builder rushed to remove the scaffolding from the walls and the centering from the arches and so to run the risk of the vaults collapsing. Many Gothic churches did collapse while they were being built or shortly after, and many of those that stood contain much more masonry than modern builders would consider necessary. But if Gothic builders were technically far behind the builders of today, they had both the imagination and the religious impetus to create some of the world's most beautiful structures.

As the Gothic Style spread, it was adapted to palaces, inns and houses, town halls, courthouses, hospitals, and almost every kind of building the people in Europe required. Such a public building as the town hall of Louvain, Belgium, erected between 1447 and 1463 and carefully restored after severe damage in World War I, was built

Cathedral of St. Peter and St. Paul in Washington, D.C.

of stone and, like a cathedral, had much exterior decoration. Houses, however, often were built of both wood and stone—half-timbered—with the pointed Gothic arch evident in the lines of the roof and the dormers.

The Gothic Style went out of fashion during the sixteenth century and almost three hundred years passed before the Gothic Revival of the nineteenth century restored it to popularity. Late in the fourteenth century, when the English cathedrals of Wells and Gloucester were still being built, a way to make cast iron was discovered in England, but cast iron did not become a building material until the end of the eighteenth century. Once the strength of cast-iron beams and girders was recognized, they were concealed behind stonework or wood to add support to the Gothic Revival structures built in the nineteenth century. Many famous cathedrals and churches were built in this way in Europe and the United States. Besides St. John the Divine, which has already been mentioned, St. Patrick's Cathedral and Trinity Church in New York City are Gothic Revival structures. In Washington, D.C., however, the Cathedral of St. Peter and St. Paul, begun in 1907, is being built stone on stone in the true Gothic manner, although the temporary scaffolding is of steel and radiant heating has been installed beneath the marble flooring.

7 The Renaissance

Before the cornerstones of western Europe's last great Gothic cathedrals had been laid, what we call the Renaissance had begun in Italy, from where it spread gradually to other countries. "Renaissance" means "rebirth," and although scholars today think of the Renaissance as a period of transition rather than a period startlingly different from the Middle Ages, many men of the time felt that they were in the midst of an exciting rediscovery of the Latin and Greek classics. The change from medieval to Renaissance period has at times been overstressed, yet there *was* change. And in architecture this resulted in many fine works.

When the Renaissance began, the great majority of people still were living on the land. Europe, however, was beginning to shift from a feudal economy based on land to our modern economy based on money, and trade was developing into international commerce, bringing to some people the wealth and leisure on which Renaissance studies and art depended.

In Italy, where the many Roman ruins were constant reminders of a significant past, the writer Petrarch (1304–1374) helped to popularize the study of the old Latin classics. This "new learning" quickly became the fashion among the nobles and the newly rich "merchant princes," whose aims and points of view were quite unlike those of medieval churchmen and feudal lords. When urban nobles and merchants began to replace the church as patrons of promising artists, works of art were to be found in public buildings and private homes, and art began to reflect some worldly influences. Names of artists who created masterpieces soon were widely known—quite the reverse of the artist's situation in medieval days—and the profession of artist offered the hope of enduring fame. Not until the middle of the nineteenth century were deserving artists again to lack prestige and patronage.

As new attitudes toward the world and new ideas about man began to circulate, the pursuit of knowledge became important and the ideal of a "universal man" grew up—a versatile man, such as Leonardo da Vinci (1452–1519), who was supremely creative in several fields of endeavor. Men found a variety of ways to express their love of beauty in the natural world, of which the church formerly had sought to make them ashamed, and scientists in their studies began to rely on observations rather than on authority. While some men, like Columbus, explored the earth, artists explored new ways of expressing the realism of the world in which they lived. Sculptors made statues that portrayed the human body more correctly than ever before, even in the Great Age of Greece. Painters discovered linear perspective and so were able to represent accurately on a flat plane a three-dimensional scene as viewed from a fixed point of sight. Architects no longer were simply master masons but were men trained in more than one of the fine arts—those arts concerned with the creation of beautiful objects. Architecture, once considered a part of medieval geometry, now was elevated to the rank of fine art and was looked upon as an art of form rather than of construction, as in the Gothic period. Nevertheless, during the Renaissance, architecture, which had been the great expression of the medieval period, gave way to painting as the most admired art.

Filippo Brunelleschi (1377–1446), one of the Renaissance's "universal men," had been trained as a silversmith, sculptor, and caster of bronze, and at the age of twenty-one had full standing in the Florentine guild of goldsmiths, to which sculptors belonged. In 1401 Brunelleschi entered a contest to design a pair of sculptured bronze doors for the north entrance of Florence's old Baptistry, but when the panels he submitted won only second place he took himself off to Rome. There he gave up further thought of being a sculptor and turned to the study of architecture and of Rome's many classical ruins.

Although he had designed no known earlier buildings, Brunelleschi in 1420 was back in Florence at work on several different structures.

Brunelleschi's dome for the Cathedral of Santa Maria del Fiore in Florence

The first to be completed (1436) was the dome of the Cathedral of Santa Maria del Fiore (St. Mary of the Flowers). As early as 1296 Florence had begun this great cathedral, 508 feet long and one of Europe's largest, but work had come to a standstill after the completion of an octagonal drum to support a huge dome over the crossing. Not since the days of Hagia Sophia had anyone attempted a large dome, let alone one that was almost 150 feet in diameter. The Florentine guild of masons had been unable to come up with a solution; no one could even figure out how to build scaffolding on the drum, the top of which was 180 feet above the floor. At last, some time after 1405, Florence held another contest, this time for the design of the dome, and Brunelleschi was the winner with a design that architects still admire as an impressive feat. Actual work did not begin, however, until 1418 or 1419.

Seen from outdoors, what Brunelleschi designed looks like an elongated dome with eight ribs, which rise almost 100 feet from the angles of the octagonal drum to the base of the cupola or lantern tower. (The top of the lantern tower is 367 feet above the nave floor.) But appearances do not tell the story. Brunelleschi did use eight main ribs, but between each he added two smaller ribs, later concealed from sight. Instead of building in the Gothic manner with centering, he invented a new method of construction and a hoisting machine capable of lifting tons of material to great heights. In this way he did away with the need for scaffolding. A dome set on a drum may rise high to dominate the skyline of a city, but a dome on a drum cannot be buttressed in the old Roman manner. Brunelleschi, therefore, opposed the thrusts of the dome with the tension of wooden rings, called chains, which he reinforced at key points with iron clasps. Tension members, when they fail, fail suddenly, but all the great domes in the past five hundred years have been set on drums and have chains for tension. Brunelleschi's chains have not failed, and his system of twenty-four ribs and reinforcements was all the support needed to hold the bricks and stones that made the inner and outer shells of his dome. When these shells were complete, the sixteen smaller ribs and chains were concealed and only the eight main ribs were left in sight. Although his structural principles were medieval, Brunelleschi's dome was a transitional step from the Gothic to the Renaissance Style of architecture, because his structural elements were hidden and because his design concentrated on the effect of classical repose that came from a smooth silhouette against the sky.

While the cathedral's dome was rising, Brunelleschi was also at work on the first building that is completely in the Renaissance Style. This was the Innocenti, Florence's Foundling Hospital or orphanage,

Façade of the Innocenti in Florence

which he designed about 1419 and which was completed in 1445. What attracted most attention was the two-story façade (the third story was a later addition), where he put his emphasis on the horizontals, just the opposite of the Gothic's stress on height. One of the characteristics of the Renaissance Style was to be a flat, horizontal skyline.

Along the length of the Foundling Hospital, to make what is called a loggia, an open gallery covered with a roof, Brunelleschi used an arcade of nine round arches supported by slender Corinthian columns set on the top step of a flight of nine shallow steps. (The two side arches are not part of this loggia.) In the second story, he used nine windows, each centered above an arch. With round arches to lead the eye from one part of the design to the next, an observer quickly recognized the separate architectural elements of arch, column, and window. But because Brunelleschi had set these in a "frame" made up

Façade of the Pazzi Chapel at the Church of Santa Croce in Florence

of steps, side pilasters, and cornice, the observer was able to grasp the whole of the building at a glance. Gone were the countless Gothic combinations that led the eye slowly from one to another of the many parts of an intricate whole. Here, instead, was a design so harmonious that all parts were subordinate to a whole.

After a thousand years of medieval churches with the Early Christian basilican plan, Brunelleschi revived the domed central-plan church when he built the small chapel that is among his greatest works. Begun about 1430 and probably completed within six years, the Pazzi family's chapel in the cloister of the Church of Santa Croce in Florence marked the Renaissance's complete break with Gothic tradition. As in an ancient temple, Brunelleschi's portico of six columns was set against the almost flat background of the front wall; supported by the columns, the simple entablature made a neat balance between vertical and horizontal lines. The Corinthian columns, the center arch modeled on one in the nave of Old St. Peter's, the pilasters of the wall, and the decorative patterns on the entablature testified to Brunelleschi's studies of old Roman buildings. Inside, he used dark-colored stonework to divide the plain almost white walls of the small nave and apse into simple geometric forms—circles, squares, rectangles, and the like—which were easy to recognize and had none of the mystery of Gothic interior detail. Over the center of the chapel he set a low dome on pendentives, which made no attempt to achieve a soaring height. With this interior, Brunelleschi established a new concept of space and line, and he set a taste that dominated the design of interiors until the end of the nineteenth century.

No bygone art can ever be re-created by people of a later period; art, inevitably, must bear the stamp of its own time. Brunelleschi was not attempting to re-create classical buildings, but from his studies of what the ancient Romans had built, he had gained a great appreciation of form. He had attempted to discover and to apply the prin-

Interior of the Pazzi Chapel

Part of the façade of the Morgan Library in New York City

ciples that classical architects had followed in achieving the forms of their buildings, and his aim was beauty of design. He might use the classical elements of round arch, Roman vault, column, pilaster, and thick walls, but Brunelleschi used these in his own way to make observers especially aware of the form of what he designed.

Brunelleschi's contemporaries made much use of his innovations, but they did not fully understand what he was trying to do, and as an architect of the early Renaissance he had no rival. Even in later centuries, his ideas have been difficult to follow, and one of the few buildings that can be traced directly to his influence is the Morgan Library in New York City, begun in 1905, the façade of which has some resemblance to that of the Pazzi Chapel.

136

During the Renaissance, people were able to build better housing for themselves and the earthly possessions they were acquiring, and the city palaces that Florentine families built were far more comfortable than medieval castles. Such a palace was designed for Cosimo de' Medici, the ruler of Florence and one of the great patrons of art, in 1444 or 1445 by the architect Michelozzo, a pupil of Brunelleschi. (In the seventeenth century it was acquired by the Riccardi family and is now called the Medici-Riccardi palace.) On the outside, the ground floor with its heavy stonework looks something like a medieval fortress, but the upper stories do not. Where a Romanesque castle stressed the verticals, here the moldings (three of them are dentil ranges) that separate one story from another and the overhanging cornice put emphasis on the horizontals. This division of the exterior

Exterior of the Medici-Riccardi palace in Florence

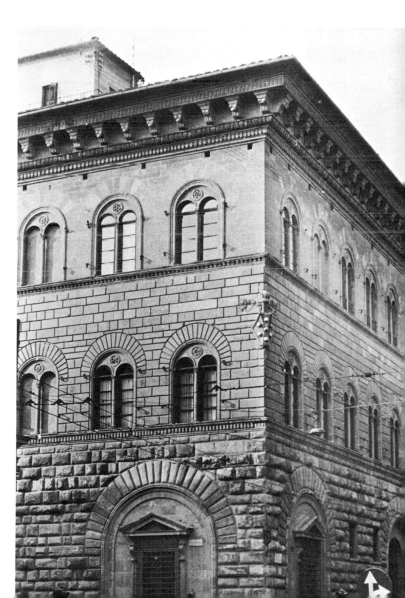

Courtyard of the Medici-Riccardi palace

of a building into distinct stories soon became a characteristic of the
Renaissance Style, and the round arches and colonettes of the upper
windows became Renaissance architectural features. Typical of the
period, the interior of the Medici-Riccardi palace was built around
an open square court, much in the manner of an old Roman dwelling.
Here for the ground floor arcade Michelozzo copied the round arches
that Brunelleschi had used on the façade of the Innocenti.

Leone Battista Alberti (1404–1472) had as much influence on Renaissance architecture as Brunelleschi, but for a different reason. Alberti
revived the form of the old Roman triumphal arch, which he incorporated into both exteriors and interiors of buildings, and like Brunel-

138

leschi he popularized the pilaster, but he influenced all Renaissance arts with his three books: *On Painting, On Sculpture,* and *On the Matter of Architecture.*

Where Brunelleschi had paid attention to the structure of his buildings as well as their design, Alberti, as he made clear in his book on architecture, thought the architect's creative responsibility was solely design. The function of an architect, he wrote, was to design a building in such a way that it conveyed to the viewer a sense of beauty and perfection. Alberti had been inspired by the newly found writings of Vitruvius, a Roman who lived in the first century after Christ and the author of the only treatise on architecture that survived from antiquity; and the closer a design came to being classical, concluded Alberti, the better it was. In his treatise, Vitruvius had written much about Greek architecture, but Vitruvius had been born almost five hundred years after the great Greek period, and when he did not know how the Greeks designed and built some structure he made up explanations. When Vitruvius was correct, Renaissance architects did not always understand what he meant, and even Alberti seems to have missed the point of what Vitruvius wrote about optical illusions in ancient Greek buildings.

One man who apparently understood what Vitruvius had meant was Donato Bramante (*c.*1444–1514), an architect who was also a painter, poet, and writer on architecture. In Rome, in 1500 1502, Bramante designed and built the Tempietto, a small circular chapel that stands in the courtyard of the Church of San Pietro in Montorio, the traditional site of the martyrdom of St. Peter. With its sixteen Doric columns, its sixteen matching pilasters on the circular wall, and its low dome (the cupola was added later), the Tempietto became for the people of Rome the ideal classical building. The Tempietto was not a copy of a classical building. What Bramante attempted to achieve were the visual effects he thought an ancient building had produced for its beholders. And he set out to attempt similar effects on a grand scale when he designed a new St. Peter's Basilica for Pope Julius II.

Rome had become the center of the Renaissance after the Medici had been exiled from Florence in 1494, and in Rome the pope and the cardinals were the great patrons of artists. During the medieval period, many Italian cathedrals had been rebuilt, but despite talk and planning, St. Peter's, the principal church of Christendom, had fallen

The Tempietto at the Church of San Pietro in Montorio, Rome

into ruins. As soon as he became pope in 1503, Julius II undertook a building program that was intended to rival those of the Roman emperors, and chose Bramante for his architect. For the large complex of buildings that Julius visualized, Bramante thought in terms of the space of the old imperial baths. He wanted to awe people in the same ways he thought those great halls had done, and for good measure he threw in the effects of the domed interior space of the Pantheon. Domes always had had symbolic meaning, and during the Renaissance some philosophers identified the dome with the heaven from which man had been expelled yet for which he continually longed.

If the interior of a dome could suggest heaven and its beauty, then the new St. Peter's should have a dome, and Bramante had to start a domed church with a central plan. The floor plan from which he worked was a large square divided into nine equal smaller squares. As the building rose, the great cubic volumes of space above these nine divisions were to merge into the climax of a low dome, like that of the Pantheon, above the center square. The cornerstone of St. Peter's was laid on April 18, 1506, but when Bramante died in 1514 only a small portion had been built. Other architects, including the painter Raphael, accomplished little except to change Bramante's plans and build models until in 1546 Michelangelo was made the architect.

Michelangelo Buonarroti (1475–1564) was truly a "universal man"— a great sculptor, a great painter, a great architect, a poet, and a writer. Except for minor changes, he adopted Bramante's original central plan and then, following Brunelleschi, he designed a high dome set on a drum to dominate Rome's skyline and make St. Peter's a symbol of the center of Christendom. Because the lower masonry that had previously been completed was not strong enough to support

Exterior of the apse and dome of St Peter's Basilica in Rome

such a dome, Michelangelo reinforced the four main piers around Bramante's center square until they were 60 feet thick. Then by means of pendentives he was able to set a circular drum above this square. Michelangelo lived only long enough to see the drum completed, but he left a large model so that others could finish it.

At the time Renaissance leadership was passing from Florence to Rome, Renaissance ideas were spreading to France. For protection, the small Italian states had made alliances with foreign countries, and so they became the scenes of warfare between France, Spain, and other rising powers. War was to ruin the Italian states, but war was largely responsible for the spread of the Renaissance. As early as 1495, when he was attempting to enforce his rights to Naples, Charles VIII of France was impressed with Italian palaces and churches. Returning home delighted with all things Italian, Charles took with him Italian architects to train French master workmen in the Renaissance Style. But love of the Gothic died hard in France, and French workmen did not like the new ways. For a time French architecture was a hodge-podge of styles, and when France did develop a Renaissance Style, it was confined mainly to chateaux, the counterparts of Italian palaces that the king and his courtiers built in the country rather than in the cities.

As the French kings grew in power and the old feudal counts and dukes became courtiers, some two hundred chateaux were built in the valley of the Loire River. The largest of these was Chambord, built by Francis I between 1519 and 1533, to provide a place for entertaining his expanding court. Francis I was a true Renaissance monarch and the patron of such Italian artists as Leonardo da Vinci, Andrea del Sarto, and Benvenuto Cellini, who lived at his court. With a round tower at each of its four corners, Chambord suggests a Norman keep more than an Italian palace, while its numerous pinnacles, chimneys, and dormer windows are Gothic details. Defense, however, was less important than comfort, and Chambord with its four hundred rooms was a large residence and not a fortress. With its long horizontal lines, its pilasters, and its cornices, Chambord is an example of the early French Renaissance Style.

In the United States, some 350 years later, George W. Vanderbilt, a grandson of the famous Commodore Cornelius Vanderbilt, began a home outside Asheville, N.C. Mr. Vanderbilt was a student and an admirer

Chambord on the Loire River

Biltmore House, outside Asheville, N.C.

of the French Renaissance Style, and the 250-room Biltmore house was designed to include many of the features of Chambord and other Loire valley chateaux. Today the house and gardens are open to the public.

The beginning of the Protestant Reformation in 1517 did not mean the end of the Italian Renaissance, but as Rome, absorbed in a religious counter-reformation, turned away from ideas from the pagan past, Venice succeeded Rome as the capital of the High Renaissance. Jacopo Sansovino (1486–1570) designed the Library of St. Mark in Venice, begun in 1536, in the accepted manner. He divided his building into two stories, a long arcaded loggia and an upper floor with deeply arched windows, and then, because the Venetians loved rich detail, he topped the upper floor with a balustrade and sculptured figures to give the Library a new skyline.

The architect whose influence was to extend far beyond Italy lived and worked mainly in the small town of Vicenza some forty miles outside Venice. In the fashion of the day, Andrea Palladio (born in 1508 or 1518) had coined his surname from that of the Greek patron of the arts, the goddess Pallas Athena. Like other Renaissance architects but even more thoroughly, he had studied Vitruvius and made drawings of the classical ruins in Rome.

Palladio's first architectural undertaking proved to be one of his most influential, although it was not completed during his lifetime. Vicenza had a great Gothic hall, called The Basilica, 173 feet long, 68 feet wide, and 80 feet high, which was used as a covered marketplace. About 1550 Palladio undertook to give this old hall a new exterior, and somewhat in the manner of Sansovino's library, he designed a two-story loggia, with nine arches on the long sides and five on the short. For the columns of the lower floor, Palladio used the Doric order, and for those above, the Ionic order, and he pierced both arcades with openings that look like portholes to create more voids for the play of light and shadow. As a whole, the exterior was not extraordinary, but the arches were. Instead of the simple arch that Brunelleschi had used in the Innocenti, Palladio combined a round-top arch with two shorter flat-top arches, one on either side, and this combination of three arches has ever since borne his name. It has been repeated thousands of times in every possible size and material until Palladian windows and Palladian doorways can be found everywhere in the Western world.

The palaces and villas that Palladio designed were quite unlike those of the early Renaissance and in time were widely copied. One of these

144

The Basilica at Vicenza

Façade of the Palazzo Chiericati at Vicenza

was the Palazzo Chiericati, built at Vicenza between 1550 and 1557. The lower columns are in the Doric order and the upper in the Ionic; the entablature is classic; and the cornice is topped with sculptured figures and vases centered on the columns below. Here, too, were windows capped with triangular pediments, another hallmark of the Renaissance Style, that Brunelleschi began with the windows of the Innocenti.

By the sixteenth century Renaissance architects were paying attention to the relationship of a building to its natural site, and Palladio's Villa Rotonda outside Vicenza, begun in 1550 or 1552, is famous for the harmony of its design and hilltop site. The Villa Rotonda takes its name from the low dome set above its central room that is 40 feet square. Like other Renaissance architects, Palladio had been influenced by the Pan-

146

theon, and the Villa Rotonda has four entrances, each with a triangular pediment supported on columns, each suggesting the Pantheon's portico. Palladio, however, set the Villa Rotonda on a podium. Until he designed the Palazzo Chiericati and the Villa Rotonda, classical columns had been reserved for churches and public structures, but with these two private residences Palladio set a fashion for domestic architecture that lasted for centuries.

As a house to live in, the Villa Rotonda was not very efficient, but its rooms were large and airy and it became a model for country houses in many places. In the United States, the best-known residence based on the Villa Rotonda is Monticello, in Charlottesville, Va., which Thomas Jefferson designed for himself. Jefferson anonymously submitted a similar design to the contest held in 1792 for a "President's House" when Washington, D.C., was being built. Although this was not accepted, the design that did win the contest and the $500 prize was by another follower of Palladio, James Hoban. The White House on its north side has a col-

Villa Rotonda outside Vicenza

Monticello in Charlottesville, Va.

umned portico topped with a triangular pediment; all its columns are Ionic; it is divided in the Renaissance manner into two stories, with the windows of the lower floor capped with triangular pediments; and the balustrade around the top is typically Renaissance.

In 1570 Palladio published *Four Books on Architecture,* the first publication to include measured drawings of ancient classical buildings and a codification of the classic orders. He also included many drawings of his own buildings and their details, which were so practical that once his books had been translated into English in 1713 even men in colonial America could build columns and porticos, doorways, windows, and moldings like those they had known in Europe.

Long before his books had been translated, Palladio's influence had brought about the decline of the Gothic Style in England. Queen Elizabeth I (1558–1603) was a Renaissance monarch, but she built no churches and was no patron of painters and sculptors. Her courtiers did not build villas or chateaux but English manor houses, which were a late Gothic development. English respect for tradition was strong, and even Inigo Jones (1573–1652), who was a great admirer of Palladio, did not abandon his use of the pointed arch until after a second visit to Italy in 1612. Seven years later Jones began to build the Banqueting Hall at Whitehall as part of a royal palace, which was never completed. Although adapted to an English setting, scaled down in size, and without emphasis on the center of its façade, the Whitehall Banqueting Hall still resembles Palladio's Palazzo Chicricati. When in 1633 Inigo Jones undertook to restore London's old St. Paul's Cathedral and was permitted to put a classic façade on this famous Gothic structure, the Renaissance Style came into favor in England. As England's first professional architect, Jones had great influence, and he and his followers were responsible for the spread of the English Renaissance Style, often referred to as the Palladian Style, because the influence of Palladio outweighed that of other Renaissance architects.

In his later years Palladio made increasing use of illusionary devices and his reason for doing so was new. Where the Greeks and some of the early Renaissance architects had used optical illusion to make the true form of their buildings obvious to the observer, Palladio sought to make what was only apparent seem real. The Church of Il Redentore in Venice, dedicated in 1576 but not completed until 1592, twelve years after his death, looks like a classical temple, but it is a basilican church, with the

149

peak of its triangular pediment equaling the peak of the center aisle inside. Behind this pediment, to either side and equal in height to the top of the side aisles, is what appears to be a second pediment of which only the end parts are visible. Such a pediment where the apex of the triangle has been omitted is called a broken pediment. Inside Il Redentore Palladio achieved an illusion of great depth by substituting for the solid wall of the apse a row of columns set in front of clear glass windows so that the eyes of the spectator were led beyond the altar to the outdoors.

West front of the Banqueting Hall in Whitehall, London

Interior of the Church of Il Redentore

By the time Palladio died, he and other architects were painting shallow plaster vaults to appear as deep barrel vaults of marble and using similar illusionary devices. The way an architect looked at design and the way an observer saw the finished building had changed radically from early Renaissance days, and the Baroque Style had come into being.

8 Baroque and Rococo

In 1519 King Charles I of Spain was made Emperor Charles V of the Holy Roman Empire and thus came to rule over the Low Countries, Austria, and what is now Germany, as well as Spain. On Sunday, May 5, 1527, Charles's mercenaries sacked Rome, making the Pope a prisoner and, according to somewhat exaggerated contemporary sources, leaving 40,000 people dead and 13,600 buildings wrecked. Three years later, after a fierce defense, Florence was forced to yield, and soon Spain, directly or indirectly, controlled all the Italian city-states except Venice.

Europe had been split by the Protestant Reformation, and the harmony of the Renaissance gave way to the tensions of a changing world. Spain for the moment was the dominant power in Europe, and Spain, like France and England, was interested in the Atlantic Ocean and not the Mediterranean Sea. As Spain grew rich on treasures from the mines of the New World and a monopoly of the spice trade, France and England waited to challenge her on the continent and on the high seas, in colonial expansion, and in trade. After the Spanish Armada was sunk in 1588, England was free to pursue her interests in North America, and France, although torn by the religious wars of 1562–1598, emerged victorious when the Thirty Years' War, fought mainly against the Holy Roman Empire, ended in 1648.

During the sixteenth century some European countries became strong centralized monarchies, and as a common religious faith and a unifying Renaissance culture disappeared, a strong sense of nationalism arose. The state—that is, the government of a country—often grew at the expense of the towns and the middle class, which had been important to both

Gothic and Renaissance developments, and governments became patrons of the arts. Almost everywhere land was at a premium. When kings sold lands that belonged to the crown to finance their wars and when the old nobility sold estates to finance the extravagant lives they led at court, the eager buyers were the people who had made their money in trade or banking. For these men, who lacked the cultural interests of Renaissance merchants, the status of lord of the manor meant social advancement. One result of this shift in land ownership was the creation of new social classes. Society now became divided into more distinct classes than during the Renaissance, and with the monarch at the top, the divisions in the social hierarchy were more rigid.

As Protestant movements spread in opposition to the Roman Catholic church, the Protestant Reformation was followed in 1534 by the Catholic Reformation, often called the Counter-Reformation. The Council of Trent, which sat from 1545 to 1563, undertook to reform the Roman church with a return to an almost medieval theology, a new definition of ecclesiastical hierarchy, new prestige for the pope, and much self-reproach for having succumbed to Renaissance influences. At the same time, science was developing rapidly, although many scientific discoveries, such as those of Copernicus and Galileo, conflicted with what the churches taught. All the world seemed to have gone to extremes, and times were tense. A taste for Renaissance grandeur remained, but much else that the Renaissance had admired was now condemned, especially pagan influences. If architecture was to express the many conflicts and contrasts of the day, it had to go in a new direction.

Baroque architects did not stop using the familiar classical elements of steps, columns, pediments, and cornices, but as inheritors of a wealth of Renaissance technical skills, they began to use these with far greater freedom than had their predecessors. They did nothing so senseless as to omit steps or put them in odd places, but the Baroque loved bigness, and architects began to pile up forms. A façade, for example, might look as though one classical temple front had been set on top of another. With sculpture and painting the favorite arts, architecture could not help being affected by these preferences. Buildings did not become settings for sculpture, as in Greek times, but architects did look at their buildings with a sculptor's eye. Sculptors must chisel away flat plane surfaces to achieve curved forms, and architects began to introduce many curves into buildings. A sculptor also is aware of the effects of light on the form he models, and in the same manner Baroque architects used some forms to catch highlights and others to make shadows. From painting, Baroque architects borrowed their concern for color and texture of building materials, and like painters they strove to create illusions, especially the illusion of depth. In time, architects, painters, and sculptors worked as teams to produce Baroque buildings that were integrations of their three arts.

Baroque architecture also responded to another development. During the second half of the sixteenth century town planning as we understand the term came into existence, and town planning in the sixteenth century was the province of the architect, who had control over a considerable area of ground as well as a variety of buildings. Then, as now, town planning put emphasis on a dramatic skyline, but where we think of skyscrapers, Baroque architects thought of domes. They built domes on drums with chains instead of buttressing, and just when they should have thought about relieving some of the weight (when the Romans put an oculus in the Pantheon's dome), they added the weight of a cupola. Cupolas were much favored by Baroque architects. Gothic builders had prided themselves on their sound construction. Baroque architects seemed often to defy construction, piling form on form deliberately to startle the observer with unusual arrangements of shapes and lines. The effect of serene balanced repose for which Renaissance architects had striven was all but forgotten.

The Rome of 1527 that Charles V had ordered sacked was a dirty, badly laid out medieval city with a population of about fifty thousand. As architect to the pope, Bramante earlier had tried to make some improvements, but not until the Council of Trent ended and Rome's population had almost doubled did the popes determine to give Rome a new dignity and beauty. Then Rome was laid out like a modern city. New bridges and wide streets were built to make the city accessible to pilgrims, and new squares, or piazzas, were added where fountains played and to which ancient obelisks were moved. By 1600 more than fifty churches and chapels had been built or restored, and Rome's skyline was dotted with domes.

Before these things were accomplished, in the first efforts to repair the damage done by the troops of Charles V, Michelangelo had designed a group of three buildings for Rome's Capitol Hill shortly before he began work on St. Peter's dome. Built between 1538 and 1561, the Palace of

Palace of the Senate in Rome

the Senate, the Palace of the Conservatori and its twin, the Capitoline Museum, belong to the period of the High Renaissance, but partly because of what he did with this group of buildings, Michelangelo has been called one of the "fathers" of the Baroque Style. Michelangelo, Sansovino, and Palladio all influenced Baroque architecture, and all three were trained as sculptors.

Michelangelo arranged the Capitol Hill buildings around a piazza in the center of which is a statue of Marcus Aurelius, the old Roman emperor. The Palace of the Senate, which has inspired thousands of other buildings, is in the middle, flanked by the other two. Michelangelo based his design for the Senate on the old Roman version of the Greek temple, but he set it on an unusually high podium and then topped it with a low balustrade instead of the high entablature the podium seemed to suggest. In the twin palaces, Michelangelo showed his disrespectful attitude toward the classic orders by demoting the columns to little more than window decoration. Where another Renaissance architect would have used columns, he used great two-story pilasters of the Colossal order, which he invented to use here. (The fact that a column or a pilaster runs through two or more stories and not absolute size determines the

Façade of the Capitoline Museum in Rome

Colossal order. Technically, the colonettes of a fireplace can be in the Colossal order if they rise through two or more horizontals.)

Buildings in groups had been designed ever since Hellenistic days but never with such success. Michelangelo invented the Colossal pilaster as a common element that would link up the three Capitol Hill buildings, which he set around an open piazza in a way that included the free space of the square in his composition. Since Michelangelo thought of himself first as a sculptor, he was more aware than most Renaissance architects of the effects of light and shade, and he arranged the three buildings deliberately so that no two receive the sun at the same time of day. Thus he anticipated much of what Baroque architecture would do with forms and startling effects and something of modern town planning.

One of the churches that was built when the popes began work on Rome's new appearance was Il Gèsu, the principal church of the new Society of Jesus, which had been founded in 1540 by the Spaniard Ignatius Loyola. This new religious order, best known as the Jesuits, had played a major role at the Council of Trent, and the Church of Il Gèsu has had a great influence on church architecture ever since Giacomo Vignola designed it during the 1560's. The Jesuits were anxious to dignify the church service and to emphasize the beauty of the ritual, but they wanted also to preach a doctrine that applied to the realities of the day. Consequently, they put emphasis on acoustics to be sure people heard the sermon, and they insisted on having enough daylight inside the church so that the congregation could both watch the gestures of the priests and follow the prayers in their missals, which by now were printed books. Accordingly, Vignola designed a church with a nave and two rows of shallow chapels in place of side aisles, which marked the return to favor of the basilican-plan church. The short transepts and the dome over the crossing were, however, in the style of Michelangelo, but in the dome were windows of clear glass to light the interior. Baroque architects were to place their sources of interior light in similar high places, almost concealed from the worshipers below. While Il Gèsu did not overthrow all the Renaissance traditions, it was a step toward the Baroque Style. Its two-story façade, completed in 1584 by Giacomo della Porta, suggests one classic temple set on top of another. And concealing the shed roofs over the two rows of side chapels were great stone volutes, much larger than those of Ionic column capitals, which would grow in popularity as the Baroque put emphasis on curved lines.

157

Façade of the Church of Il Gèsu in Rome

Since Michelangelo's death in 1564, little work had been done on St. Peter's, but on his election in 1585 the energetic Pope Sixtus V put men to work day and night and Sunday, and completed the dome in twenty-two months. Although he had Michelangelo's large model to follow, Giacomo della Porta, who became the new architect of St. Peter's, gave the dome a steeper pitch than Michelangelo had intended, and he built the lantern tower so high that its tip is 452 feet above the floor. As a result, St. Peter's was the tallest building in the world until the Eiffel Tower was built in Paris in 1889. And St. Peter's soon became also the world's largest building.

In 1605, under orders from Pope Paul V, the remains of Old St. Peter's finally were torn down, and the next year Carlo Maderno (1556–1629) went to work to complete the new St. Peter's. Before he could design the façade that won in a competition, Maderno had several problems to solve. The Pope wanted St. Peter's to be a basilican church suitable for long processions, and he also wanted an exterior place from which to bestow his blessing on the world. Michelangelo's central or Greek-cross plan was out of favor because it suggested the pagan side of the Renaissance, yet whatever he did Maderno knew he must not spoil the effects of Michelangelo's great dome. To make St. Peter's into a basilican church, Maderno extended the nave westward by adding three bays. At the same time he made the nave wider and higher and lighted it with windows. The results were quite different from what Michelangelo had intended. For the façade, Maderno used all the traditional elements, but where Michelangelo had planned pilasters, he used huge

St. Peter's Basilica and St. Peter's Square, with the Vatican in the right background

columns spaced at irregular intervals. He did use a low pediment, much like the one Michelangelo designed, and beneath this is the balconied window of the Benediction Loggia where the pope appears. Instead of the balustrade Michelangelo had intended, Maderno built an upper story topped with a balustrade and accented at either end with a low bell tower. Nothing interferes with the view of Michelangelo's dome, and with its play of light and shadow the Baroque façade has an effect of movement and depth. Unlike a Renaissance architect, Maderno gave little thought to the temples of antiquity when he designed St. Peter's façade. Although he retained a long horizontal line with the entablature, he put his emphasis on the center of the façade, and he grouped the masses of the great columns to give an exciting rather than a serene effect.

Gothic cathedrals were built quite naturally in the midst of city houses, but as Baroque architects strove to separate their buildings from the immediate surroundings, they artificially molded the space of a setting into their architectural designs. Such a setting was created for St. Peter's in 1656–1663 by Gian Lorenzo Bernini (1598–1680), who designed the piazza into which thousands of people crowd on special church occasions. Around an oval-shaped area, Bernini curved the two arms of a double colonnaded walk, so that space, colonnade, and St. Peter's seem to be molded into one whole.

As a boy of fifteen, Francesco Borromini (1599–1667), a contemporary of Bernini, ran away from home to work under Maderno on St. Peter's façade. As a Baroque artist seeking new forms, Borromini concentrated on walls. Where the Gothic architect had cut away straight walls when striving for height and light, Borromini altered the structure of a straight wall so that a convex surface was followed by a concave one. The effect was of something fluid, like the crest of a wave and its trough, yet Borromini's structures were as sound as Gothic cathedrals. When Borromini designed the small monastic Church of San Carlo alle Quattro Fontane (St. Charles of the Four Fountains), he made the nave in the shape of an ellipse and used sixteen Corinthian columns to lead the eyes of the observer along the curves to the curved altar. His Church of Sant' Agnese in the Piazza Navone, designed in 1652, is sometimes said to typify Baroque church architecture. Its façade, considered one of the most beautiful Baroque façades in Rome, has walls that curve inward from two bell towers, which have steeples topped with stone imitations of small Chinese caps.

Façade of the Church of Sant' Agnese in Rome

Between 1658 and 1670 Bernini built the Church of Sant' Andrea al Quirinale for the Jesuit novices in Rome. Although his simple façade uses columns, pilasters, and a triangular pediment, the effect is far more sophisticated than that of a Renaissance building, and the whole had been carefully planned in relation to the street that it faces. The plan of this small church is in the shape of an oval, around the rim of which are eight chapels. The main chapel is set off by four columns, and above

Interior of the Church of Sant' Andrea al Quirinale

the architrave the pediment has been hollowed out to hold a statue of
St. Andrew after his martyrdom being carried to heaven, which is represented by the cupola above. From unseen sources in the cupola, light
pours on the interior and the altars.

Bernini was a sculptor, a painter, and a dramatist as well as an architect, and Sant' Andrea al Quirinale is a good example of the Baroque
union of the arts. By this time Italian architects designed Baroque
churches much as a modern stage designer designs settings for a play.
The tunnel vaults of the nave and apse were painted to give the illusion
of great depth; the dome interior was painted to give the illusion of souls
being wafted upward; sculptured figures of angels and saints floated on
stucco clouds; and sometimes singers were concealed around the dome

162

to give worshipers the illusion of heavenly voices! Rome in the seventeenth century had regained much of its old reputation as an art center, and artists from other countries, often under government subsidy, went there to study and to copy Italian masterpieces. The influence of the classical past was still great, but before the century was over Paris had become the art capital of the world.

Paris began to grow into the "queen of cities" when Henry IV, who ruled France from 1589 to 1610, set out to make his capital a beautiful city. Like the popes in Rome, Henry IV planned on a large scale, and Paris developed great squares surrounded by residential or public buildings, wide connecting avenues, and many bridges over the Seine. In much the same way, the capital city of Washington, D.C., was planned by another Frenchman in 1791. Pierre Charles L'Enfant was a major under Lafayette in the American Revolution, and the broad streets radiating from many parks and squares that he designed for Washington owe much to the plan of Paris.

Louis XIV, Henry IV's grandson who ruled from 1643 to 1715, came as close as anyone has to being an absolute monarch. After 1661, when he dispensed with a prime minister, he was certainly the most important individual in Europe, and in France he centralized in himself all financial, all military, and all judicial power, and he also ruled over French culture. As a symbol of such supremacy, Louis XIV decided to build a new capital outside Paris and selected from lands belonging to the crown a wooded site where a small chateau had served his father, Louis XIII, as a hunting lodge. Begun in 1661 on an area half the size of Paris, the buildings and gardens of Versailles were laid out according to a complicated but symmetrical plan, with boulevards and paths, canals and pools, even trees and shrubbery focusing on the palace of this grand monarch. Versailles is the largest palace in the world and its gardens are the most extensive, with twelve hundred fountains and countless statues. In the course of some twenty-five years, nearly thirty thousand workmen had a hand in Versailles, including France's greatest artists. Here in 1683 Louis XIV moved his government, so that with the royal family, courtiers, guards, servants, government workers, and clergy, nearly ten thousand people were housed in the seventeen-acre palace.

Versailles, however, was not planned all at one time. The first work of enlarging the old chateau was carried out by Louis Le Vau, but with each victory of his armies Louis XIV called for an addition. To symbolize the victories over Spain and Franche-Compté, Jules Hardouin Mansart, who became the architect in 1678, added two great wings, to make Versailles 1,935 feet wide, more than a quarter of a mile. On the garden façades of these wings, Mansart treated classical columns in the Baroque way and made use of much decoration, but the horizontal division of the stories and the low balustrade with sculptures showed the continuing influence of Palladio.

Versailles was probably the most expensive palace in the world, because the setting that Louis XIV demanded for himself was elaborately decorated with paintings and murals, mirrors and tapestries, sculptures, crystal chandeliers, and other rich furnishings that included enameled silver chairs. Much as in an Italian Baroque church, all the arts were integrated inside Versailles, and the craftsmanship was of the best, although today the results seem very ornate. Just as Louis XIV was the model for other absolute monarchs, Versailles was the model for other European palaces. Louis XIV set France's taste in art, in decoration, and in manners, and what the French court did was imitated by the aristocracy elsewhere.

Part of the garden façade of the Palace of Versailles

When Cardinal Richelieu was Louis XIII's chief minister in 1624–1642, he made Frenchmen aware of the excellence of their language, the growth of their science, the high quality of their crafts, and the superiority of their taste in all the arts. He founded the Academy of Language and Literature in 1635, and soon France had academies of science, of painting, and of architecture, all of which set high standards and made sure nothing French would be undermined by foreign influences. The idea grew up in France that the arts were primarily intellectual, and therefore were best appreciated by educated people who would respond with reason rather than emotion.

Despite the grandeur of its court, France had remained a peasant country, with cities too far apart for easy communication of ideas. The Renaissance Style of architecture had never filled France's needs, and France had clung to its Gothic traditions. Although Italian Baroque developments affected them to some extent, French arts more and more were influenced by the decisions of its academies and by artists sent to Rome to study the classical past. As a result, France developed a style of architecture called the Classic Baroque, which was more rigid and more formal than that of Italy.

In 1665, Louis XIV had summoned Bernini to Paris to redesign the palace of the Louvre (now a museum), and during Bernini's two-year stay almost everything went wrong. Bernini was an Italian, of whom French artists were jealous, but, more important, Louis XIV considered Bernini's first design too curved and rejected his others as unpractical or expensive. When an eastern façade, nearly 600 feet long, for the Louvre was undertaken in 1667, its designers were Frenchmen: the architect Louis Le Vau, the painter Charles Le Brun, and Claude Perrault, who had been trained first as a physician. Some things about the Louvre façade resemble Michelangelo's Palace of the Senate; the balustrade is Palladian; and the flat skyline, which was new in France, came from Bernini's plan. The effect of the long colonnade of Corinthian columns set in pairs on a high podium is more classical than anything done in Renaissance Italy, but the Baroque influence is evident in the centered pediment and in the space provided between the colonnade and the wall to create a play of light and shadow.

The classic direction of French Baroque can be seen in the Church of Les Invalides, designed by J. H. Mansart in 1706 to complete the retreat for infirm soldiers that Louis XIV had built in Paris. Instead of the exuberance of Italian Baroque, the columns and walls of this Greek-cross church show a restrained treatment, but the façade is set forward to allow for a play of light and shadow. Like St. Peter's, the dome of Les Invalides has had wide influence. Because the body of Napoleon was later interred in Les Invalides, its interior was used as a model for the interior of the tomb built on Riverside Drive in New York City for General Ulysses S. Grant in 1892–1897.

In England, the middle class did not lose its power as in the countries on the continent, and although London was the capital, London in the seventeenth century was a middle-class city, with the nobility residing elsewhere. The idea of the divine right of kings had come to an abrupt end when Charles I was beheaded in 1649, and Charles II had no thoughts of becoming an absolute monarch when he was restored to the throne in 1660, even though he had been at the court of Louis XIV. The bubonic plague that depopulated London in 1664–1665 was followed in 1666 by the Great Fire, which raged for days, destroying eighty-eight churches and thirteen thousand dwellings and shops along four hundred streets. When it came to rebuilding London, Charles II had neither the power nor the wealth of Louis XIV, but he did have as his deputy surveyor-general Christopher Wren (1632–1723), a mathe-

East façade of the Louvre in Paris

Façade of the Church of Les Invalides in Paris

matician turned architect. And Wren had recently returned from a visit to Paris where he had had long talks with French architects and had met Bernini.

Wren was given the job of laying out a large part of London—he was made surveyor-general in 1669—and the plan he made called for a series of squares and radiating streets at the center of which was to be a new St. Paul's Cathedral. To give the city a definite skyline, he proposed to build at certain key points churches with spires so that the dome of St. Paul's would stand out as the main point of interest. Old St. Paul's, remodeled by Inigo Jones, had been so damaged by the fire that it could not be salvaged, and Wren thus was able to plan a new city around its cleared site. Backed by the power of neither a pope nor an absolute monarch, Wren could only watch helplessly while the ap-

167

Façade of St. Paul's Cathedral in London

proaches to this site on Ludgate Hill became a clutter of buildings shopkeepers and householders rushed to erect. One after another his plans for St. Paul's failed to win approval, and nine years went by before the cornerstone was laid on June 21, 1675.

Christopher Wren might appreciate Baroque developments, but Londoners associated foreign styles of architecture with court extravagances, and the Church of England detested anything associated with Roman Catholicism. The clergy of St. Paul's leaned toward a Gothic cathedral with a long nave and side aisles, but they did like the space associated with a Palladian building. Wren had to scrap first his plan for a centralized church in the tradition of Bramante and Michelangelo

168

and then his favorite plan for a church with curved walls. At last the authorities settled on a Latin-cross plan for a church with a wide nave and a low dome over the crossing to be topped with a tall steeple. Wren, however, was given leeway to make modifications if they were necessary, and during the forty years it took him to build St. Paul's he managed to make quite a few "necessary" changes.

The accepted plans called for a façade with columns of the Colossal order, but no quarry could be found to supply that length of stone. Wren, therefore, redesigned the façade so that it had two stories and used six pairs of Corinthian columns below and four pairs above. This façade suggests both a Roman classic temple and the Baroque churches of Italy, and the twin towers with their steeples have much in common with those of Borromini's Church of Sant' Agnese. Behind the façade can be seen St. Paul's enormous dome. Because St. Paul's, like so much of London, is built on a site where solid ground is buried under 40 feet of sand and clay, Wren was ever aware that he must lighten the weight of his great building as much as possible. Yet, as time passed, he substituted for the low dome and steeple of the accepted plan an immense dome set on a drum and topped with a tall cupola, which alone weighs 800 tons. Engineers and architects have ever since marveled at the ingenious ways he devised to make this possible and sound. Inside, St. Paul's is laid out much like a Gothic cathedral, with three aisles, transept, choir, and apse. On the outside, the walls are divided into two stories, where the columns, pilasters, triangular pediments of windows, and balustrade suggest the Renaissance and Palladio, while the dome resembles that of Bramante's Tempietto. It took a Baroque architect to combine a Gothic floor plan with Renaissance taste and classic forms, and St. Paul's is called a "Baroque synthesis."

Like the dome of St. Peter's and of Les Invalides, the dome of St. Paul's influenced the design of many later domed buildings. In the United States, the capitols of several states are descendants of these domed structures, and certainly the dome of the Capitol in Washington is related to them also.

Christopher Wren lived to be ninety-one years old, and he never stopped working and inventing. When he drew up his plan for London, the decision had been to rebuild fifty-one of the eighty-eight churches that had burned, and by 1700 Wren had completed forty of these besides working on St. Paul's. Each parish church had to be small, be-

Capitol of the United States in Washington, D.C.

cause money was scarce, yet Wren did not skimp and each had a different design. Once again, Wren's leanings toward the Baroque ran head on into the parishioners' taste for the Gothic, especially for Gothic spires. As a result, Wren worked out a compromise, and a number of these churches have classical façades, above the horizontal of which rises the vertical of a steeple. Wren paid much attention to the design of his steeples. One of his most famous is that of St. Mary-le-Bow, where the famous Bow bells hang. There the steeple rises rhythmically from a square base through several rounded stages to an eight-sided pyramidal spire. Any abrupt change from one geometric form to the next was concealed by Baroque volutes and twists and by Renaissance balustrades and columns. James Gibbs (1683–1754) continued the building of churches in the Wren tradition, and the churches of these two English architects were the models the colonists sought to imitate when they built churches in the new towns and cities of America.

In the colony of Virginia, Williamsburg was laid out as the capital city with as much care as the capitals in Europe. At the western end of

Duke of Gloucester Street is the capitol and, facing it, at the eastern end of the street is the College of William and Mary, chartered in 1693. There, now called the "Wren Building," is the oldest academic building in the United States. Although the plans were altered to adapt it to the site, contemporary sources say that this building was "first modelled by Sir Christopher Wren." Little about it suggests a Baroque synthesis. Wren never visited Virginia, but by a turn of fortune, the United States has a genuine Christopher Wren church.

St. Mary Aldermanbury, which Wren completed in 1677, was one of the parish churches designed after the Great Fire of London. Unlike St. Paul's Cathedral, which miraculously stood almost untouched during the bombings of World War II, this church was badly damaged in 1941. When London came to rebuild after the war, the site was needed for other purposes, and the rest of St. Mary Aldermanbury was torn down and its pieces shipped to Westminster College, Fulton, Mo., where on March 5, 1946, Sir Winston Churchill had made his famous

Interior of the Church of St. Mary Aldermanbury before it was bombed

"Iron Curtain" speech. Although the rebuilding according to Wren's original plans was not complete, the dedication of St. Mary Aldermanbury in the fall of 1966 celebrated both the twentieth anniversary of Churchill's speech and the three hundredth anniversary of the Great Fire of London.

The Rococo Style began in Paris in protest at the formality of the court at Versailles. The Rococo grew directly out of the Baroque, but where the Baroque was large and massive, the Rococo was light and delicate; where the Baroque tried to make an emotional impact, the Rococo tried to charm the observer. As a result, the Rococo developed as an interior style for houses rather than an exterior style for palaces and public buildings, but its appeal was wide.

The word "rococo" may have been coined from *rocailles* (rockwork, pebbles) and *coquilles* (shells), two forms that the new style used, or it may be a pun on the Italian word for "baroque," which is *barococo*. Whatever the derivation of the word, as the eighteenth century passed, rocks, shells, and similar curved shapes appeared on wallpapers, fabrics, mantlepieces, silverware, and pieces of furniture as well as ceilings and walls. The Rococo Style of decoration was taken up by the court of Louis XV (reigned 1715–1774), and furniture of the period is sometimes referred to as being in the style of Louis Quinze.

The Thirty Years' War (1618–1648) had been especially disastrous for Austria and Germany, where the destruction was enormous, but even after that war ended peace did not come to central Europe until the Turks had been defeated at the siege of Vienna in 1683. As a result, the Baroque came late to this region, yet both Austria and Germany eventually made contributions to that style and to the Rococo.

In the cities, Italian and French influences were strong, and where people were affected by the Catholic Reformation, they rebuilt their churches in the Italian Baroque Style. In Vienna, the Karlskirche, the Church of St. Charles Borromeo, begun in 1715, was based on Borromini's Church of St. Charles of the Four Fountains, but the architect Johann Bernard Fischer von Erlach gave it an unusually wide façade and made an innovation with the triumphal columns. When he designed the garden façade of the Belvedere Palace (in Italian architecture, a *belvedere* was a building overlooking a fine view), Lukas von Hildebrandt had Versailles in mind, but his pediment does not suggest a classic one and his decorations show no Palladian restraint.

Façade of the Karlskirche in Vienna

In the country, where the people had suffered enormously and many monasteries had been destroyed, architecture reflected the tastes of the peasant people who did the rebuilding rather than aristocratic influences from abroad, and the Pilgrimage Church at Vierzehnheiligen, built between 1743 and 1772, is an example of the appeal that the Rococo had for people everywhere.

The idea of beauty had had a strong influence on all Renaissance arts, but as time passed beauty in architecture seemed to have been forgotten. The Baroque grew in ornateness and the Rococo verged on mere prettiness, but political events rather than aesthetics put an end to both. In the wake of the American and French revolutions and the

Interior of the Pilgrimage Church at Vierzehnheiligen

rise of Napoleon, architectural styles associated with a way of life that had come to be detested were discarded. Today the forces that created the Baroque Style are understood, and the great accomplishments of Baroque architects are respected—perhaps because the tensions and divisions that brought it into being are not too different from those of our own time.

174

9 The Nineteenth and Twentieth Centuries

The Rococo was the last style of Western architecture to have wide acceptance, and the aristocrats were the last international group of art patrons. When it came to be identified in the minds of the people as the style of a decadent upper class, the Rococo abruptly went out of favor near the end of the eighteenth century. Since then no new architectural development has had sufficiently wide acceptance to become an international style, although the contributions of individual architects have been significant and influential.

Over the centuries, art and architecture had been successively under the patronage of the great rulers, the church, merchant princes, kings, and then the aristocracy. Wherever they had the means to do so, European aristocrats had followed what was in fashion, but even before the French Revolution the aristocracy was losing its power and popularity if not its heads. The French Revolution was followed almost immediately by the rise of Napoleon, and the countries of Europe as they armed to protect themselves against Napoleon's ambitions, became increasingly nationalistic. So, too, did the new United States. Tendencies toward specialization in the arts began to grow, and as the arts took on national rather than international characteristics, artists became specialists in a single field and no longer were the masters of all the arts as in Renaissance and Baroque times.

More important than the American and French revolutions was the spreading Industrial Revolution, with its vast social and economic changes. As industry grew and commerce in manufactured goods expanded, the middle class acquired wealth, but middle-class people did not replace the aristocrats as patrons of the arts. The nineteenth century saw important literary developments, especially in the novel and poetry, and in France the contributions to painting were significant. But the painters who made these contributions were not recognized by their own generations, and after centuries of fame and fortune the career of artist no longer carried prestige. Here and there, a few men were patrons of individual artists, but the average solid citizen of the nineteenth century frankly disliked the creative arts of his own day. With painters and sculptors so misunderstood, architects were not likely to go against the tastes of their clients to develop a new style. Yet new architectural needs were arising everywhere.

Building problems had remained the same for centuries. Religious groups had needed temples or churches; governments had needed administrative buildings and town halls; kings and nobles had needed castles and palaces; and the people had needed some kind of shelter. By the nineteenth century, a new way of life brought about by the Industrial Revolution had need for factories and workshops, for railroad stations and power plants, and buildings soon had to include the technical developments of indoor plumbing, electricity, and the telephone. But in the nineteenth century the great need in Europe and the United States was for housing. As the century began, no one foresaw that population would increase enormously. In the United States between 1800 and World War I, the population grew from about five million to almost a hundred and six million and in England from nine million to forty-one million. And no one foresaw that as industry became mechanized, so many people would shift from farming to work in city factories and offices. For thousands of years the great majority of people had lived on the land, but by the end of World War I the majority of people in the United States and in some European countries lived in cities, many of them crowded into dismal tenements. As cities grew and factories multiplied, cities were faced with the need to separate industrial from residential areas, and city planning, even regional planning, became more important than ever before.

As the nineteenth century began, the first answer to the need for new buildings surprisingly came in the form of another revival of the classical styles of architecture. This nineteenth-century enthusiasm for the ancient styles of Greece and Rome was not the same as that during the Renaissance, because neoclassicism—new classicism—was the choice of the

176

people and not just of the educated upper classes. Before the French Revolution two apparently insignificant happenings had had enormous effects on the attitude of people in general toward art and architecture. The first of these was the excavation, begun in 1748 (and still continuing), of Pompeii and Herculaneum in Italy. News of the excavations was followed eagerly in periodicals and books, and the French in particular were startled to learn just how comfortably middle-class people had lived in these ancient resort towns. Once the French Revolution made it possible, classicism, which previously had meant temples and grand monuments, was associated in the minds of the people with an unpretentious but luxurious domestic architecture, something worth striving for.

The second happening was the publication of two books on ancient art. For ten years two Englishmen, James Stuart and Nicholas Revett, had traveled in Italy and Greece, examining and measuring ancient Greek buildings, in particular those on the Athenian acropolis. When the first part of this monumental work, *The Antiquities of Athens,* appeared in 1762, it included accurately scaled drawings, and the authors distinguished between Greek and Roman architecture. The German scholar J. J. Winckelmann went one step farther, and in his *History of the Art of Ancient Times,* published in 1764, said that Greek art was better than Roman. Two hundred years ago few facts were known about the ancient works of art and people were so eager to learn that Winckelmann's book became something like a modern best seller. Winckelmann made a number of mistakes when he identified and dated artists and works of art, but his influence as an art historian was enormous. Scholars for the first time began to study systematically the classical art of Greece and Rome, then the art of the Renaissance, and in the second half of the nineteenth century, the medieval styles. Winckelmann's writings also set the taste of people in the late eighteenth and early nineteenth centuries, who soon were admiring all earlier art indiscriminately.

Napoleon admired almost everything about the old Roman Empire, and when he came to power he set out to replan Paris with new monuments and vistas, much as the Roman emperors had done in ancient Rome. Military victories called for new buildings, and soon Paris had two triumphal arches, a monumental column imitating Trajan's in his Forum, and the Church of the Madeleine, which on the outside looks like the old Maison Carrée at Nîmes. France and the countries under its

A Greek Revival house in a New England town

domination favored the revival of the Roman Style, while England and
Germany, France's sworn enemies, understandably preferred Greek
Revival buildings with flat surfaces, colonnades, and triangular pediments. In the United States, although Thomas Jefferson admired the old
domed Pantheon, most people preferred the Greek Revival, which began
about 1830.

In England, the Gothic Style had been revived late in the eighteenth century by a few wealthy gentlemen who wanted country residences that looked like medieval abbeys. Influenced by the romantic literature of the early nineteenth century, people began to build Gothic villas, and when the new Houses of Parliament were begun in 1839 the Gothic Revival had triumphed over the classical. As the influence of the Houses of Parliament was felt, architects turned more and more to the Gothic Revival Style for important public structures, churches, and university buildings. Many newly rich people in both England and the United States, as a result of the prosperity created by the Industrial Revolution, sought to live their private lives in romantic settings, and Gothic Revival houses sprouted pointed arches and gables, spires, and imitation battlements, while their interiors imitated in plaster and even papier-mâché the Gothic decorations that centuries before had been perfected in stone. Now the property of the National Trust for Historic Preservations and open to the public, Lyndhurst in Tarrytown, N.Y., was designed in 1838.

Houses of Parliament, as seen from the River Thames, London

West façade of Lyndhurst, a Gothic Revival mansion in Tarrytown, N.Y.

by Alexander Jackson Davis, a Gothic Revival architect, as a Hudson River country retreat for a New York City politician. In Germany, the Gothic Revival appeared in the form of rural castles. In France, it resulted in the careful restoration of some of the great buildings destroyed during the Revolution. Unfortunately, enthusiasm for the Gothic led to disastrous remodeling of some of Europe's older buildings, especially churches.

The Gothic Revival was not entirely bad. While architects had little understanding of the needs that had given rise to the original style, and while it was impossible to train men in the skills of the medieval mason, Gothic Revival structures were soundly built. And Gothic Revival

180

houses were responsible for new house plans. Up to this time almost every house had a symmetrical plan, with two rectangular or square rooms on either side of a one-story center hall. In the Gothic Revival period, some houses had assymetrical plans where circular or hexagonal rooms were fitted in with square and rectangular ones. Such innovations were to have future significance, but in the middle nineteenth century irregular house plans most often stemmed from the whim of a client or the peculiarities of a site and not a new architectural philosophy.

With no architectural traditions of its own and much new money to spend, the United States was especially receptive to the successive revivals of the historic styles. Greek, Gothic, Italian Renaissance, Romanesque, the Greek again, Rococo, even Egyptian, and the Gothic again in the late Victorian period—each received nationwide enthusiasm. Town halls, jails, courts and colleges, armories and libraries, churches, and houses were built in whatever was the latest fashion, no matter how inappropriate. One style revival followed so closely on another that no native American architecture had a chance to develop, and architects specialized in one style as long as it was popular.

As the nineteenth century passed, however, art historians completed their studies of the historical styles, and both photography and the printing processes developed to where photographs could be reproduced as printed book illustrations. Thus well before the end of the century architects became familiar with almost every famous building in the world, and some architects became eclectic. This meant that they selected elements from several styles instead of just one, but they did not combine them in a single building as Sir Christopher Wren had when he made St. Paul's Cathedral a Baroque synthesis. Instead, architects, with staffs of draftsmen to help them, were able to design in several styles simultaneously: a French Renaissance chateau for this client, a Romanesque armory and a Gothic Revival church for others.

Throughout the nineteenth century, the function of the architect was much discussed. Was he a designer or an engineer, artist or builder? Architects who thought of themselves as artists and designers were sufficiently influential, especially in the United States, to set the tastes of their clients. Today it seems absurd, but at that time many people thought that the Greek Revival Style was most appropriate for banks, because columns and pediments suggested dignity and stability; Gothic or Romanesque Revival was the choice for churches; Renaissance

Revival was considered appropriate for office buildings; and Roman baths were good for railroad stations.

While much nineteenth-century architecture was historical make-believe, the Industrial Revolution brought about changes in production methods and the development of new building materials. And with new materials, structural systems that had existed in theory became realities. With steel, other metals, reinforced concrete, and glass, architects for the first time in history were not limited to natural building materials, and new materials set architects searching for new forms and new decoration. More important for people in general, the search for new architectural forms grew out of architects' awareness that contemporary needs could not be filled adequately by borrowings from the past.

The development of cast iron at the end of the eighteenth century seemed to offer great possibilities. A puddling process for wrought iron made possible such structures as suspension bridges, and one of the earliest (1822–1826) appears in the photograph of Conway Castle. But iron was neither a practical nor an economical building material until Sir Henry Bessemer in 1855 discovered a process for converting iron into steel. Cast iron will rust. Although it will not burn, it is affected by high temperatures, and although it has strength in compression, it has low tensile strength—that is, strength to withstand tension. While steel will rust, and is affected by very high temperatures, it is lighter in weight than iron and has both compressive and tensile strength. As a building material, cast iron is ugly, but it had been used in the early nineteenth century for some factories, where people in those days did not care about appearances, and for the girders and beams concealed behind masonry or wood. Then in 1851 cast iron and glass were used in a most unusual building.

Much as he would have designed a giant greenhouse, Joseph Paxton, an English landscape gardener, designed the Crystal Palace as the main exhibition hall for the Great Exhibition of the Works of Industry of All Nations, which opened in London in 1851. Although the arches over the center aisle spanned only 70 feet, the Crystal Palace was 408 feet wide and 1,851 feet long, in recognition of the year the Exhibition opened, and only four months had been needed to erect a building covering eighteen acres. Instead of the familiar mass of masonry, the Crystal Palace was a network of iron columns, girders, and trusses bolted together and sheathed with eighteen thousand panes of glass, which

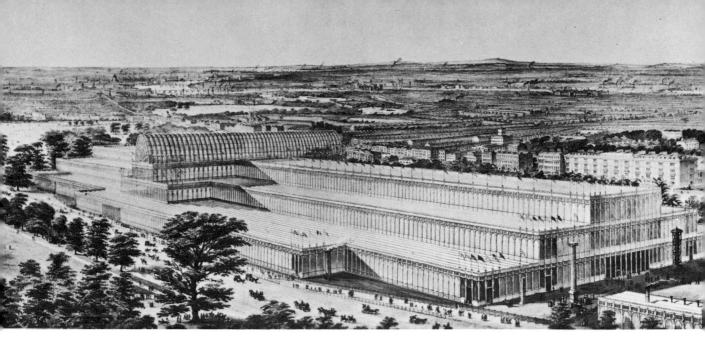

Exterior of the Crystal Palace in London, from a contemporary lithograph

previously had been put into prefabricated sections for speedy assembly. The result was both impressive and exciting. (In 1854 the Crystal Palace was moved to a new site, where it served as a museum until 1941 when it was demolished because it had become an obvious landmark for German bombers.)

Using only iron parts that had been standardized like those of the Crystal Palace, Gustave Eiffel, a French bridge engineer, built the now-famous Eiffel Tower for the Paris International Exhibition of 1889. Made of thousands of small parts riveted together, the Eiffel Tower stands more than 1,000 feet high, a monument to nineteenth-century architectural engineering and a frank display of structure and material.

Once steel could be produced at a reasonable cost and in sufficiently great lengths, the steel skeleton or steel frame became possible, and the first steel-frame building, the Home Insurance Building, was erected in Chicago in 1885, four years before the Eiffel Tower. Steel-frame construction is simply a variation of the old post-and-lintel system, but the steel skeleton made possible the modern skyscraper.

For several decades people had been experimenting with ways of building a sound structure of more than four stories, but the first really tall building was not erected until 1890–1891. This was the nine-story Wainwright Building in St. Louis, Mo., designed by Louis Sullivan

(1856–1924), a Chicago architect, and it was Sullivan who coined the word "skyscraper." At this time, what was called the "Chicago window," with large panes of glass, was being developed to let much light into the interior of a building and make possible display windows in ground-floor shops. Using this window, D. H. Burnham and J. W. Root in 1894 redesigned the four-story Reliance Building they had begun in Chicago in 1890 and made it into a fifteen-story skyscraper. When all the weight of a building is supported by its steel frame, walls no longer carry any load or thrust, and the glass of the Crystal Palace and of the Chicago windows of the Reliance Building were forerunners of the "glass skin" found today on so many buildings.

Despite the innovations made in Chicago, their wide acceptance was postponed by the influence of the eclectic architects. Tall buildings might have steel frames to carry the stresses and strains, but the taste for the Revival styles was so strong that tall buildings went right on being sheathed in masonry with Renaissance, Gothic, Romanesque, or classic details. Gothic was thought especially appropriate for skyscrapers —witness the 792-foot-high Woolworth Building, designed by Cass Gilbert and erected in 1911–1913, which for almost twenty years was the world's tallest building. By the 1920's, however, this eclecticism was being questioned as more and more people became aware that contemporary means existed to serve contemporary architectural needs.

Some of Louis Sullivan's theories about architecture were as important as the buildings he designed, and one of his ideas was that "form ever follows function." By this he meant that the shape of a building—its form—should suggest to the observer the function it served, the work that went on inside. Consequently, he believed that buildings should be

The Reliance Building in Chicago

The Woolworth Building in New York City

designed from the inside out, and the form of his skyscrapers, of story piled on story, grew out of his having considered first the shops that would be on the ground floor and the dozens of offices that would occupy the upper floors. Interpreting Sullivan's ideas for themselves, later architects said that if form was to follow function, materials should be used honestly. Stone should behave like stone, steel like steel, and the way the steel frame of a building performed its function should not be concealed by a coating of stone. It took time for these architects to gain their point, but eventually skyscrapers became open structures with their steel frames sheathed in glass, the obvious descendants of the Eiffel Tower and the Crystal Palace.

When land is at a premium, as it is in most cities, skyscrapers and tall apartment buildings become a necessity—provided that their sites are firm enough to support them. No one can afford to spread a one-story building over a large site, and to be economical city buildings must rise vertically. Skyscrapers certainly are functional in that they provide well-lighted working space for many people, but the stark form of the modern skyscraper is not always admired. One building that sometimes is considered an exception is Lever House, built in New York City in 1952 by the architectural firm of Skidmore, Owings & Merrill. Here, half the building site was sacrificed so that the verticals of the skyscraper part of Lever House could be offset by the long horizontal of the low base. The base was made into an open passageway for pedestrians, a garden, and a glassed-in art gallery, which were possible because Lever House has no ground floor. It is cantilevered outward from the steel shafts on which it rests.

A cantilever is a projection, usually a beam, that is supported at only one end, and cantilevering is the structural system whereby the load-carrying beams are projected beyond their supports, in the way a shelf is projected out from a wall when supported on brackets. To be efficient, a cantilever must be made of material of great tensile strength, and cantilevering of any size had to wait for modern building materials.

Before World War I, architects in several European countries, influenced by Sullivan's ideas, were designing functional buildings along similar lines. Out of the work of such men as J. P. Oud in Holland, Le Corbusier in France, and Gropius and Mies van der Rohe in Germany came the so-called "International Style" of architecture, which is largely associated with cantilevered steel-skeleton buildings with glass skins. Walter Gropius (1883–   ) had built glass-and-steel factories in Germany as early as 1914, but his most influential project was the Bauhaus buildings at Dessau, Germany, built between 1925 and 1929 to house studios, offices, living quarters, and a workshop for a machine-age experiment in the training of young artists. For the various buildings, Gropius

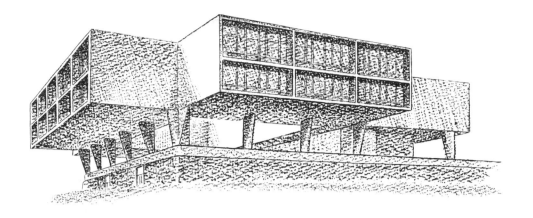

An example of cantilevering

Lever House in New York City

A corner of the Bauhaus workshop in Dessau

thought of space as contained in "boxes" or cubes of varying size, and when he built the "box" that was to be the workshop he cantilevered it out from its base. The glass walls frankly expose the beams and uprights of the frame, and the stairway shows clearly through the walls. From the Bauhaus to Lever House was no great step.

The term "International Style" is misleading, because the architects associated with it do not work in identical ways. Ludwig Mies van der Rohe (1886–   ) has made much use of glass as a building material, but his concept of space is not quite the same as Gropius'. In the 1920's he designed houses in which the space for living was clearly separated from the space for service activities, and both his designs and his use of "space dividers" instead of solid walls have had great influence. Since 1938 Mies van der Rohe has lived in the United States, and besides Chicago apartment houses and a New York skyscraper, he designed

Crown Hall at Illinois Institute of Technology, Chicago

Crown Hall for Illinois Institute of Technology's Institute of Design and departments of architecture and city and regional planning. This is a one-room building, unobstructed by columns or posts, made possible by a load-bearing frame that passes above the roof. Le Corbusier (1887– 1965), whose real name was Charles-Edouard Jeanneret-Gris, was born in Switzerland, lived in Paris after 1917, and worked in South America and Asia as well as Europe. In his early designs, he put an even greater emphasis on geometric form than did Gropius. This pure geometry combined with his definition of a house as a "machine for living in" resulted in buildings that many people found cold and forbidding, such as the villa at Garches, a suburb of Paris near Versailles. In his later designs, however, Le Corbusier turned toward less rigid forms when he designed the Chapel of Notre Dame du Haut at Ronchamp, France, the Center of Visual Arts at Harvard University, and the government buildings at Chandigarh, the capital of the Punjab.

Reinforced concrete was Le Corbusier's favorite building material.

With the fall of the Roman Empire concrete disappeared from Europe, and not until the middle of the eighteenth century was the method of making hydraulic cement rediscovered. But as a building material, modern concrete had to wait until Portland cement, patented in 1824, was produced commercially. Today concrete is made by mixing gravel, sand, water, and Portland cement, almost the same mixture the Romans made. By itself, concrete is not so strong as stone, because it is weak in tension, but as the Romans knew, concrete can be poured into molds. When steel rods, metal bars, wires, or metal frameworks are placed in the molds before the concrete is poured, the hardened mixture has the compressive and tensile strengths of steel. Such a mixture is called reinforced concrete or ferroconcrete and was developed soon after commercial Portland cement. Concrete and metal expand and contract at about the same rate during temperature changes, and by the last decade of the nineteenth century a structural basis for the use of reinforced concrete had been worked out by the Frenchman François Hennebique.

Once reinforced concrete was accepted as a building material, it opened up many possibilities for straightforward architectural forms, because it could be poured into molds of almost any shape. Anatole de Baudot invented some new decorations, but he also imitated Gothic

Villa at Garches

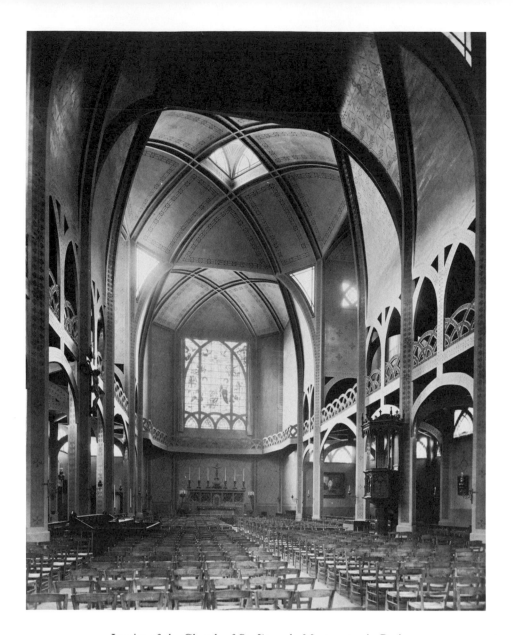

Interior of the Church of St. Jean de Montmartre in Paris

stone vaults when in 1894 he designed St. Jean de Montmartre in Paris, the first church made of reinforced concrete. Since then, this man-made material has been used in practically every kind of building and to make many imaginative as well as borrowed shapes.

Frank Lloyd Wright (1869–1959) was nineteen years old when he went to work in 1888 for the Chicago architectural firm of Sullivan

& Adler. Although he remained there only six years and thereafter practiced independently, he was much influenced by Louis Sullivan's ideas, which he interpreted very differently from the Internationalists. Sullivan had used the term "organic building" to differentiate his architecture from the designs of eclectic architects who borrowed from the historic styles. What "organic building" meant to Sullivan is difficult to define, but to Wright the term meant that architecture should be as creative as nature and that the inner nature of an architectural problem would eventually suggest the problem's solution. In contrast to the Internationalists, whose buildings sometimes seem to defy nature, Wright insisted on the harmony of a building to its natural site. He did not believe in tailoring nature into an artificial setting for a building, as Renaissance and Baroque artists had, because he felt a house should be identified clearly with its natural setting. He thought that the natural materials of stone and wood were the best building materials, and—most important—his first consideration was the needs and the feelings of the people who would occupy the buildings he designed. As Sullivan had done with his skyscrapers, Wright designed a house from the inside out, with no regard for the traditional forms. He detested a house that looked like a "box with holes punched in it," and he despised eclectic architecture, which he called "façade-making." Glass-and-steel skyscrapers and other open buildings he referred to as "indecent architectural exposure."

Wright began putting his ideas into practice in city houses in Chicago. One of these, built in 1902, was the Willitts House, which he designed in the form of a cross. From a central fireplace, four wings projected out among the trees and lawns blending the house into its setting. In this and other early houses, Wright used projecting horizontal roofs to unify house to site, and sometimes he had only one or two principal rooms that could be divided into living areas, instead of several rooms some of which were seldom used. In these and other ways Wright developed a new way of molding space within a house, but his ideas shocked most people in the United States at the time when the eclectic architects were so influential. Europe, however, was ready for Wright's ideas.

The Crystal Palace was a sensation, but the Great Exhibition it had housed in 1851 was a source of concern to some people, who saw in the hundreds of machine-made exhibits only a confusion of forms and

Willitts House in Highland Park, Ill.

inferior workmanship. Largely to protest the effects of mass production on the design of furniture and decorations, William Morris (1834–1896) founded the Arts and Crafts Movement to restore England's old simple handicrafts and the use of natural materials. The decay of form, he felt, might lead to the decay of all human values if people surrounded themselves with decorations in poor taste. At that time people lived in houses with heavily curtained small windows and filled their dark rooms with heavy reproductions of furniture in past styles and a clutter of Gothic Revival knickknacks. Morris, who was famous as a poet and painter, had had some training as an architect. In 1859, when he decided on a new house, he approved a design by Philip Webb that now is recognized as a new approach to domestic architecture. Designed roughly in the shape of an L, the layout of Red House was unsymmetrical, with two sitting rooms to the left of the entrance and a dining room on the right, behind which was the kitchen. Not only was the plan unconventional, but the simple brick exterior and plain interior were a far cry from the stucco exteriors and ornate interiors that were popular in that day. Before Sullivan was old enough to put his ideas into words, Morris had built a house that had been planned from the inside outward.

By the end of the nineteenth century, English architects were assuming responsibility for the design of furniture and decorations to suit the houses they designed, and houses began to show a new treatment of space. The two-story hall now became popular, with rooms on both floors grouped around the hall as the activities of the occupants suggested. Influenced by England, countries on the continent were feeling their ways toward contemporary architecture for contemporary needs. Houses with two-story living rooms appeared, such as the villa at Garches, and furniture was made in new designs. The European architects who built houses were enormously receptive to Frank Lloyd Wright's ways of molding interior space, although some did not agree with his architectural philosophy. Eventually, by the 1930's, the United States was affected by the contemporary developments in Europe and at last recognized that Frank Lloyd Wright was one of the great pioneers of modern architecture.

Throughout his long career, Wright remained an individualist with a tremendous imagination. He continued his preference for working with natural materials, but in 1936, when he built what is probably his best-known house, he used reinforced concrete for the first time.

Red House at Bexley Heath, Kent

Falling Water at Bear Run, Pa.

Falling Water, a residence in a dramatic site at Bear Run, Pa., has two great concrete horizontal terraces cantilevered over two ledges of natural rock and a waterfall, but the vertical central core of the house was made of ashlar—huge, squared blocks of stone.

In 1936 Wright also began the administration building of the Johnson wax company at Racine, Wis. There the vast space of the main office is broken by rows of inverted columns, which taper downward from great umbrellalike "capitals" to small steel bases. Wright's attitude toward the age-old classical column was even more disrespectful than Michelangelo's.

With the destruction of cities during World War II and the subsequent population explosion, building problems have multiplied, but so have building opportunities. More than ever, today's architects have a sense of responsibility to mankind, and planning for the future reaches beyond cities and suburbs into planning for whole regions.

Some people live near architectural masterpieces and some live in towns and cities where the past is very recent. But old or new, large or small, the buildings you see are the result of men's efforts to build something more than a practical shelter.

Glossary

ABACUS: the flat upper part of the capital of a column. In the Doric style it is square with straight sides; in other styles it may be shaped or molded.

ACROPOLIS: the fortified hilltop of a Greek or Asia Minor city.

AMBULATORY: a sheltered walk, such as the walk around a Greek temple or the aisle around the apse of a church.

APSE: in a church, a projecting area at one end, usually the eastern, and usually semicircular in shape.

APSIDAL CHAPELS: small, usually very shallow chapels built in the apse along its outer rim.

ARCADE: a row of arches supported on columns or piers.

ARCH, TRIUMPHAL: originally a Roman free-standing structure through which victorious generals led a procession of captives and booty; later the large arch framing the apse of a Christian church.

ARCH, TRUE: a curved supporting or ornamental structure over an opening. It is made of wedge-shaped pieces placed at right angles to the curve and resting on supports at each end. An arch must be built on a temporary center support, which cannot be removed until the arch and its permanent supports are completed.

ARCHITRAVE: the beam, or lowest division of an entablature. It rests on the columns and supports the frieze.

ATRIUM: an open courtyard, surrounded by covered arcades, in front of an Early Christian church (derived from the court or principal room in a Roman house).

ATTIC: the masonry block above an arch.

BAILEY: 1. the outer wall of a feudal castle. 2. also the space enclosed by it.

BARREL VAULT: an arched (semicircular) roof or ceiling.

BASILICA: 1. an oblong Roman public hall. 2. an oblong Christian church.

BAS RELIEF: in sculpture, carving that projects only slightly from the background, as distinguished from either high relief or sculpture in the round.

BAY: 1. a principal compartment or division, set off by pillars, etc. 2. an alcove, sometimes projecting from a building, as a bay window.

BOSS: the ornamental knoblike part at the intersection of Gothic vaulting ribs.

BROKEN PEDIMENT: a pediment that omits the apex of the triangle.

BUTTRESS: a side support for an arch or wall, usually a wall that might be pushed over by the weight it carries. A buttress, as distinguished from a pier, does not carry the weight directly.

CANTILEVER: a horizontal beam that is anchored like a diving board at one end, supported at some point along its length, and carries a load at the other, projecting, end.

CAPITAL: the uppermost part of a column or pilaster.

CARYATID: a sculptured female figure used as a column.

CELLA: the main, inner room of a Greek or Roman temple.

CENTERING: the temporary structure, usually of wood, over which an arch is built.

CHAIN: wooden rings that resist the outward pressure of a dome built on a drum.

CHANCEL: the part of a church containing the altar and reserved for the choir and clergy, sometimes screened off.

CHEVET: the apse of a French Gothic cathedral with a series of scallops for chapels along the semicircle.

CHEVRON: a zigzag decoration used by the Normans.

CLERESTORY (sometimes spelled CLEARSTORY): the upper part of a hall that is taller than the other parts of a building (as the nave of a church is taller than the aisles). It illuminates the entire interior through windows that are higher than the roofs of the lower parts.

COFFER: an ornamental recessed panel in a ceiling, vault, or dome.

COLONNADE: a series of columns set at regular intervals.

COLONETTE: a slender half column attached to a wall or to a main column.

COLOSSAL ORDER: any order of column or pilaster that extends through more than one story or horizontal division.

COLUMN: an upright supporting member, usually cylindrical in form and usually made up of a base, a shaft, and a capital.

COMPLEX OF BUILDINGS: a group of buildings related by purpose or style.

COMPRESSION: the strain on building materials that are being squeezed by the weight they bear—as opposed to *tension,* the strain of pulling.

CORBEL: a projecting piece of masonry, wood, or metal designed as a support.

CORINTHIAN ORDER: the last and most ornate of three Greek orders of architecture. Its column was slender and its capital was decorated with acanthus leaves.

CORNICE: the uppermost division (usually projecting) of an entablature.

COURSE: a row of bricks or masonry blocks extending the length and thickness of a wall.

CROSS VAULT: the vault that is made when two barrel vaults intersect at right angles to each other.

CROSSING: the place in a church where the transept crosses the nave.

CRUCIFORM: in the shape of a cross.

CUPOLA: a small domelike roof or, loosely, a small domelike structure built on top of a roof.

DENTIL RANGE: a row of small blocks often ornamenting the cornice in the Ionic and Corinthian orders.

DOME: a roughly hemispherical roof.

DORIC ORDER: the earliest and simplest of three Greek orders of architecture. Its column was heavy and its capital was basin-shaped.

DRUM: 1. one of the drum-shaped segments that make up the shaft of a column (fluting was carved after the drums were erected into a column). 2. a cylindrical wall used as a base for a dome.

ECHINUS: the curved molding under the abacus of a Doric capital.
ENGAGED COLUMN: a column attached to a wall.
ENTABLATURE: the upper unit of a classic order of architecture; it is supported by columns and divided horizontally into architrave (bottom), frieze (middle), and cornice (top).
ENTASIS: in a column that tapers toward its capital, a slight swelling in the curve of the taper—if the taper were straight, the sides of the column would seem from a distance to curve toward each other at the middle.
EXTRADOS: the top curve or face of an arch.

FACADE: a Renaissance word for the principal face or front of a building.
FACING: any material used to cover or coat the outside of a structure, as marble over brick.
FLECHE: a slender tower erected above the crossing of a church or cathedral.
FLUTE: one of a series of regularly spaced vertical grooves of a classic column.
FORUM: a Roman marketplace or public place for legal and business matters.
FRIEZE: 1. the middle horizontal section of an entablature, often having sculptured decoration. 2. any band of sculpture or ornament, especially on a wall.

GALLERY: a long narrow corridor, sometimes at the level of an upper floor.
GROIN: the curved line formed by the intersection of two vaults.

HIGH RELIEF: in sculpture, carving that projects considerably from the background, as distinguished from either bas relief or sculpture in the round.
HYPOSTYLE: having a flat roof that rests on rows of columns (especially used of Egyptian architecture).

INTRADOS: the bottom curve or face of an arch.
IONIC ORDER: the second of three Greek orders of architecture. Its column was slender and its capital had ornamental scrolls (volutes).

KEEP: a relatively recent word for the stronghold or inner tower of a medieval castle.
KEYSTONE: at the crown of an arch the center voussoir or block that is said to bind the whole arch.

LANTERN: a cupola or tower containing windows.
LINEAR PERSPECTIVE: a method of drawing a picture so that it has a highly realistic appearance of depth. Artists long knew that in a picture, say, of two similar objects, they could make one seem farther away by drawing it smaller. With linear perspective (developed during the Renaissance) they were able to figure out exactly how much smaller, and thus to handle complex scenes with sureness and accuracy.
LOGGIA: a roofed arcade generally attached to or forming a part of a building.

MASONRY: 1. the craft of working or building with stone, brick, plaster, etc. 2. something built by a mason.

MATRONEUM: an upper gallery of a building, usually a church, reserved for the use of women.

METOPE: in a Doric frieze, which is composed of alternating rectangles called triglyphs and metopes, a metope is a square space often ornamented with sculpture.

MONOLITH: a large stone or single block of stone.

MORTAR: a semiliquid mixture used with bricks or stones to bind them together when it hardens.

MOSAIC: a surface decoration on a floor, wall or ceiling, made of small pieces of colored glass, stone, etc.

MOTTE: a steep earthwork mound or a hill on which a castle was built.

NARTHEX: originally, the portico (entrance porch) of an ancient temple; later, the porch or lobby leading into the nave of a church.

NAVE: in a church, the main hall, not including the side aisles. It often has a clerestory. In a basilican church it extends from the entrance to the choir or chapel; in a cruciform church, from the entrance to the crossing.

OBELISK: a four-sided stone pillar, usually a monolith, that tapers to a pyramidal point.

OCULUS: a hole (or eye), as at the top of a dome, through which light enters.

OGIVE: 1. the rib or groin of a cross vault. 2. often incorrectly used to refer to a Gothic, or pointed, arch.

ORDER OF ARCHITECTURE: a system of columns and the entablature they support. The Greeks developed the famous Doric, Ionic, and Corinthian orders.

PARAPET: a low wall at the edge of a terrace or roof. On a castle, a parapet was made high enough to protect men on the walk behind.

PEDIMENT: 1. the triangular area, sometimes containing sculpture, between the entablature and the roof of a Greek or Roman temple. 2. a triangular unit used as decoration, as over a doorway or window.

PENDENTIVE: a piece of masonry in the shape of a spherical triangle (a triangle cut from a sphere), used to help support a dome on piers or columns (rather than on a cylindrical wall with few openings as in the Pantheon), thus allowing free access to the space beneath the dome. A dome might crack if supported at only a few points, but pendentives support the entire rim.

PERISTYLE: a succession of columns surrounding a building or a court.

PIER: a solid vertical mass, used as a support. It may be either free-standing, like a column, or built into a wall. Compare with buttress, which does not support any weight.

PILASTER: the projecting part of a rectangular pier that is attached to a wall and made to look somewhat like a column by being given a capital, and sometimes fluting.

PODIUM: a low foundation wall or terrace.

PORTAL: a door, a gate, or, often, an impressive entrance.

PORTICO: a colonnaded porch of a building, often with entablature and pediment, and approached by a flight of steps.

POST AND LINTEL: a system of two uprights (columns or piers) supporting a beam over an opening.

SARSEN: the name given to any one of the sandstone uprights at Stonehenge.

SCULPTURE IN THE ROUND: a free-standing carved figure, as opposed to either high relief or bas relief.

SHAFT: the part of a column between base and capital.

SQUINCH: an arch or lintel built across a corner to help support a dome or other superstructure.

STATICS: the branch of mechanics that treats of the balance of weights and forces.

STOA: in ancient Greece, a sheltered promenade with colonnaded front and walled back.

STYLOBATE: a floor or base supporting a row of columns.

SYMMETRY: a balanced appearance achieved in architecture usually by making one half of a façade look more or less like the mirror image of the other side.

TENSILE STRENGTH: the ability of a material to resist stretching or being pulled apart.

THRUST: outward pressure, as when the pressure of weight on an arch results in pressure outward from the sides of the arch.

TRACERY: ornamental stonework, spreading out like branches, found on Gothic windows.

TRANSEPT: in a cruciform church, the part that crosses at right angles to the nave.

TRIFORIUM: a gallery above the side aisles of a church, making an upper story from which one can look down into the nave. If there is a clerestory, its windows are above the triforium.

TRIGLYPH: in a Doric frieze, which is composed of alternating rectangles called triglyphs and metopes, a triglyph is a projecting area ornamented with three vertical grooves.

TRUSS: a rigid framework used to support a roof or bridge.

VAULT: an arched roof or ceiling constructed of stone, concrete, or brick.

VOID: the space between two solids, of interest because it can contribute variety to the surface of a building.

VOLUTE: a decorative scroll, especially of an Ionic capital.

VOUSSOIR: one of the wedge-shaped pieces that make up an arch.

Index

Roman numbers indicate illustrations

212

    218

Sources of Illustration

Drawings by John King

The photographs on the pages indicated came from the following sources:
Alinari, Florence: pp. 50, 74, 133, 134, 135, 161, 162
Alinari-Anderson, Florence: pp. 68, 72, 81
Anderson, W. J., and Spiers, R. P., *Architecture of Ancient Rome,* published by B. T. Batsford, London, in 1927: p. 58
Archives Photographiques, Paris: pp. 59, 89, 90, 91, 93, 96, 100, 105, 108, 110, 113, 115, 116, 123, 143, 164, 166, 167, 184
Austrian State Tourist Dept., New York City: p. 173

Barsotti, F., Florence: p. 138
Biltmore Company, The, Asheville, N. C.: p. 143
Böhm, Osvaldo, Venice: p. 151
British Travel Association, New York City: pp. 24, 102, 103, 168, 179

Cathedral Church of St. John the Divine, New York City: p. 104
Chase, The Rev. Loring D., Washington, D.C.: p. 41
Chevojon Frères, Paris: p. 192
Chicago Architectural Photographing Co., Chicago, Ill.: pp. 185, 194
Conant, Kenneth J., Cambridge, Mass.: p. 71
Columbia University, New York City: p. 62

Deutscher Kunstverlag, Munich: p. 82

Ewing Galloway, New York City: p. 18

French Cultural Services, New York City: pp. 117, 120
French Government Tourist Office, New York City: p. 52

Gabinetto Fotographico Nazionale, Rome: p. 158
Giraudon, Paris: p. 125
Gropius, Walter, Cambridge, Mass.: p. 189

Hedrick-Blessing, Chicago, Ill.: p. 196
Hervé, Lucien, Paris: p. 191
Hirmer Verlag, Munich: pp. 79, 174

Illinois Institute of Technology, Chicago, Ill.: p. 190
Italian Institute of Culture, New York City: pp. 75, 94
Italian State Tourist Office, New York City: pp. 54, 60, 159

Jefferson, Thomas, Memorial Foundation, Charlottesville, Va.: p. 148

Kersting, A. F., London: pp. 98, 99, 119, 155, 156
King, John, New Canaan, Conn.: pp. 44, 51, 82, 131, 136, 137, 178, 186

Lever Brothers Co., New York City: p. 188

McKenna, Rollie, Stonington, Conn.: pp. 145, 146, 147
Metropolitan Museum of Art, New York City, Purchase, 1890, Levi Hale
Willard Bequest: p. 22
Manthoulis, Robert, Greece: p. 37

Nash, Haghe, and Roberts, *The Great Exhibition:* p. 183
National Monuments Record, London: pp. 150, 171, 195
National Trust for Historic Preservation, Washington, D.C., Library of
Congress photo: p. 180

Pitkin Pictorials Ltd., London: p. 122

Soprintendenza, Rome: p. 140
Staatliche Museen zu Berlin, Berlin: p. 43
Straussman, Arnold D., Glen Rock, N.J.: pp. 32, 39, 40
Streifus, Esther J., Hartsdale, N.Y.: p. 38

United Arab Republic Tourist Office, New York City: pp. 14, 19, 21
United States Department of the Interior, National Park Service, Washington, D.C.: pp. 26, 45, 170

Vatican Photographic Archive, Rome: p. 141

Washington Cathedral, Washington, D.C.: p. 127
Wright, Hamilton, Organization, Inc., New York City: p. 12